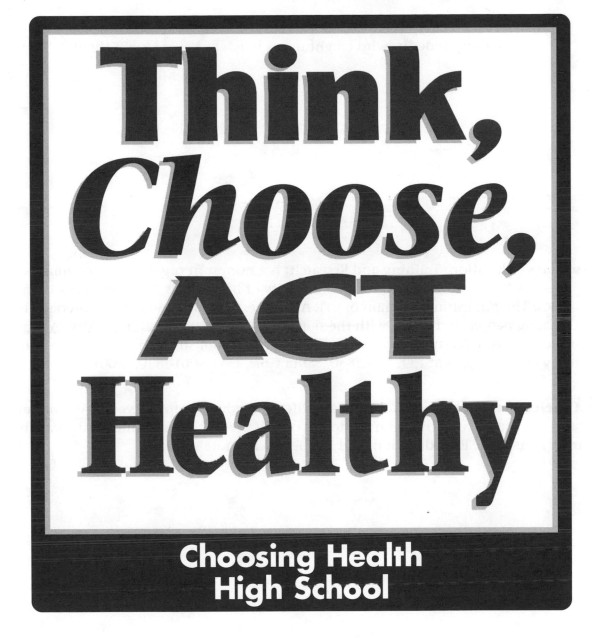

Think, Choose, ACT Healthy

Choosing Health
High School

Hilda Clarice Quiroz

ETR Associates
Santa Cruz, California

1997

For all my students, who taught me as much as I ever taught them.

— Miss Q

ETR Associates (Education, Training and Research) is a nonprofit organization committed to fostering the health, well-being and cultural diversity of individuals, families, schools and communities. The publishing program of ETR Associates provides books and materials that empower young people and adults with the skills to make positive health choices. We invite health professionals to learn more about our high-quality publishing, training and research programs by contacting us at P.O. Box 1830, Santa Cruz, CA 95061-1830, (800) 321-4407

Hilda Clarice Quiroz has been a health and life-skills educator for 20 years. As a national consultant, she presents trainings on the topics of HIV prevention education, cultural diversity and comprehensive health education, and has been a keynote speaker.

© 1997 ETR Associates
All rights reserved. Published by ETR Associates,
P.O. Box 1830, Santa Cruz, CA 95061-1830

Printed in the United States of America

10 9 8 7 6 5 4 3 2 1

Design and Illustrations: Charlene Grondahl

Title No. H688

ISBN 1-56071-526-X

Table of Contents

Strategy Descriptions

Activities

Abstinence

Table of Contents

Body Image and Eating Disorders

Table of Contents

Communication and Self-Esteem

Fitness and Health

Table of Contents

HIV and STD

Sexuality and Relationships

(continued)

Table of Contents

Sexuality and Relationships *(continued)*

Tobacco, Alcohol and Drugs

Table of Contents

Violence and Injury

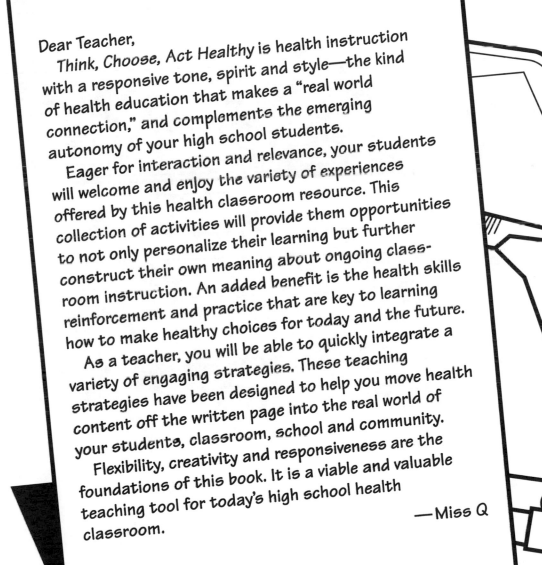

Dear Teacher,

Think, Choose, Act Healthy is health instruction with a responsive tone, spirit and style—the kind of health education that makes a "real world connection," and complements the emerging autonomy of your high school students.

Eager for interaction and relevance, your students will welcome and enjoy the variety of experiences offered by this health classroom resource. This collection of activities will provide them opportunities to not only personalize their learning but further construct their own meaning about ongoing classroom instruction. An added benefit is the health skills reinforcement and practice that are key to learning how to make healthy choices for today and the future.

As a teacher, you will be able to quickly integrate a variety of engaging strategies. These teaching strategies have been designed to help you move health content off the written page into the real world of your students, classroom, school and community.

Flexibility, creativity and responsiveness are the foundations of this book. It is a viable and valuable teaching tool for today's high school health classroom.

—Miss Q

Introduction

Think, Choose, Act Healthy is a collection of highly engaging learning strategies designed to extend students' critical thinking and health skills practice around a variety of today's hottest classroom health topics.

HIGH SCHOOL KIDS LIKE IT BECAUSE...

- Its activities are springboards for "real world thinking."
- There is room for diversity of student thought, opinion and experience.
- The activities encourage students to experience and exercise their "power" as health advocates.
- The activities are interactive, challenging and creative—qualities that make learning interesting and fun.

TEACHERS LIKE IT BECAUSE...

- The activities are flexible and responsive to the challenging content of today's high school health curricula.
- The collection of strategies support and sharpen critical thinking and problem-solving skills.
- Every activity is an opportunity for health skills practice.
- The pace of the instruction is quick and energizing.
- Overall, it is a resource that helps to realize quality and effective health instruction in today's high school classroom.

HOW THIS BOOK IS ORGANIZED

The book opens with the strategy descriptions section. Here, you are provided with a "thumbnail" sketch of each of the 14 strategies contained in the book. The approximate time the activity will take and the materials you will need are listed.

The book is then organized into 8 topics of instruction that reflect the current Centers for Disease Control and Prevention (CDC) priority areas for health instruction. These instructional topics are Abstinence; Body Image and Eating Disorders; Communication and Self-Esteem; Fitness and Health; HIV and STD; Sexuality and Relationships; Tobacco, Alcohol and Drugs; and Violence and Injury. The activities pages are presented as masters to be duplicated as needed for instruction. The corner tag on each page identifies the specific subject covered by the activity.

How you decide to use the activities to introduce, support or extend instruction within each area will determine the order in which you use them.

Introduction

ABOUT HEALTH SKILLS INSTRUCTION

Each of the strategy descriptions includes a specific health skill theme integral to the learning experience. Identified along with these themes are the various sub-skills to be learned and practiced during the activity. These key skills themes and their significance to meaningful and quality health instruction are described below.

Assessing Personal Health and Risks

Before students can take action to protect themselves from risks to health and safety, they need to have knowledge about themselves personally, in addition to knowledge about the potential risks related to a behavior. They also need the skills to assess health risks and to perceive themselves at risk.

Gathering and Assessing Health Information

Locating sources of health information, accessing that information and evaluating the validity of the information are all critical to empower individuals to take healthy action.

Rewarding Healthy Behavior

The ability to sustain the practice of healthy behavior is in large part dependent on experiencing successful results when that behavior is practiced. Feeling good about a behavior increases the likelihood that an individual will continue to practice the behavior.

Communicating with Others

Communication is an essential prevention skill. Students who have developed effective communication skills can establish a feeling of connectiveness; express their feelings, needs and desires; communicate their health needs; and resist internal or external pressures to practice unhealthy behaviors.

Negotiating for Health

Pressure from peers, societal norms and the influence of advertising are often in conflict with personal, family and cultural norms and the practice of healthy behavior. Students need to be able to negotiate the right and the opportunities to practice healthy behavior. Negotiating for health is more than communicating what you want; it involves resisting pressures to choose options that are inconsistent with personal, family or cultural values.

Health Skill
Negotiating
for Health

Making Decisions

When combined with health knowledge and the opportunity to make healthy choices, the ability to make decisions is a powerful skill. Students need to be able to identify decision points, clarify complex issues, gather information, evaluate the advantages and disadvantages of alternatives, and take action. This ability moves students closer to good health.

Health Skill
Making
Decisions

Managing Stress

Stress is part of everyone's daily routine. Although we commonly think of stress as a result of negative events, stress results from positive events as well. The ability to deal with stressful situations without jeopardizing one's health is an essential skill. Students need to be able to identify situations that cause stress and minimize its potentially harmful effects.

Health Skill
Managing
Stress

Setting and Achieving Goals

The ability to create opportunities and to set and achieve goals is important to practicing healthy behavior. Students who can identify their needs, set goals, and take action to achieve those goals are able to take charge of creating their own opportunities to practice healthy behaviors.

Health Skill
Setting and
Achieving Goals

Introduction

HOW TO USE THIS BOOK

Think, Choose, Act Healthy works best in a classroom atmosphere of mutual trust and respect, student to student and student to teacher. Established groundrules regarding sensitivity and confidentiality are a must.

Prior to Instruction

- Thoroughly review the strategy background information and the individual strategy and decide whether it will be used to introduce, reinforce or extend instruction.

- Make any required modifications that will support or respect the special needs of your students.

- Prepare needed materials.

During Instruction

- Invite divergent or creative thought and model respect for diversity of culture, opinion and experience.

- Move the strategy with a quick and engaging pace.

- Revise the strategy as needed.

After the Instruction

- Process the learning experience with your students.

- Repeat the use of a particular strategy across the various content areas to help instill a sense of familiarity and predictability for your students around a learning experience and the expectation for their performance.

Strategy Descriptions

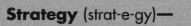

Strategy (strat-e-gy)—
A plan for maneuvering mental forces into the most advantageous position for learning, prior to, during or after engagement with key subject matter content or concepts. A goal for making a "real world" connection, building esteem and instilling a sense of empowerment in your students.

Question Roll Call

Time
10 minutes

Materials
• Roll call question of the day

WHAT IS IT?

It's a "quick-prompt" question that engages each and every student within the first 10 minutes of class. It helps you to learn and respect what students know, think and feel about a subject before instruction begins. Students enjoy listening to the thinking and reasoning of their peers. This begins the processes of exploring peer norms and personalizing learning.

HOW TO DO IT

Step 1: Review the list of topic questions. Select and modify your choice as required to meet your students' needs and the amount of time available for responses.

Step 2: Write the selected question on the board. Ask students to think about how they will respond.

Step 3: Call roll, allowing students to answer the question in response.

Step 4: Process and provide appropriate closure for the activity.

KEY SKILLS TO BE LEARNED AND PRACTICED

Health Skill
Communicating with Others

- expressing oneself verbally and nonverbally
- listening, processing and clarifying verbal and nonverbal communications
- responding to verbal and nonverbal requests
- accepting differences between oneself and others
- identifying and overcoming communication barriers

Time
20–30 minutes

Materials
• 1 activity sheet
  per student

WHAT IS IT?

It's a thought-provoking way to introduce a unit of study. Simple yet creative readings set the stage for students to explore and address the emotions, attitudes, challenges and issues related to a given topic. The activity leaves room for students to begin to fit themselves into the learning picture as they think critically and begin to look for the personal relevance of the upcoming topics of study.

HOW TO DO IT

Step 1: Review the selected reading. Modify as needed.

Step 2: Take a few moments to project your students' "first reactions" and the issues you expect will be generated by the reading. Prepare to align students' possible concerns, interests and insights with the upcoming unit of study.

Step 3: Allow students to complete the reading on their own. Then read it aloud as a class.

Step 4: Begin discussion by requesting initial reactions to the reading. Continue by asking students to identify a list of the critical issues they believe surround the reading topic.

Step 5: Use student-generated insights and issues to introduce the upcoming unit of study as it relates to the given topic. Provide appropriate closure for the activity.

KEY SKILLS TO BE LEARNED AND PRACTICED

● comprehending written material

● listening and processing verbal exchanges

● evaluating information

● comparing with other sources of information

● validating a personal sense of reality

Health Skill
Gathering and
Assessing
Health
Information

Signs of the Times

Time
20–25 minutes

Materials
• 1 activity sheet per student

WHAT IS IT?

It's an invitation to students to create an "instant" bulletin board that reflects their own understanding of a subject. In only a few minutes, student thinking related to the current topic of study can be introduced, validated, corrected factually, reinforced or extended. The activity models respect for the diversity of student knowledge, opinion and experience.

HOW TO DO IT

Step 1: Review the selected bulletin board project. Modify as needed.

Step 2: Have students complete their activity sheet and contribution to the class bulletin board.

Step 3: Display student work on a prepared bulletin board.

Step 4: Process the learning by reviewing student work. Clarify any myths and make factual corrections. Provide appropriate closure for the activity.

KEY SKILLS TO BE LEARNED AND PRACTICED

Health Skill
Gathering and Assessing Health Information

- clarifying personal health knowledge, beliefs and values
- articulating personal, family cultural beliefs and needs
- listening to the ideas of others
- comparing and contrasting differing points of view
- evaluating health information
- clarifying common health myths
- projecting future scenarios

Handwriting on the Wall

Time
20–30 minutes

Materials
• 1 activity sheet per group

WHAT IS IT?

It's another instant bulletin board, and an invitation for student groups to collaborate on exploring the depth and meaning of a basic concept related to the current unit of study. The activity takes minimal time to complete, but yields high-interest results. The creation of the class bulletin board honors the diversity of student thought and allows students to help create their own learning environment.

HOW TO DO IT

Step 1: Review the activity concept prompt. Modify as needed.

Step 2: Put students into collaborative working groups of 3–4.

Step 3: Have groups complete their activity sheet and contribution to the class bulletin board.

Step 4: Post the results on a prepared bulletin board and invite students to talk about their work.

Step 5: Process and provide appropriate closure for the activity.

KEY SKILLS TO BE LEARNED AND PRACTICED

Health Skill
Communicating with Others

● clarifying personal health knowledge, beliefs and values

● expressing oneself verbally and nonverbally

● listening to the ideas and opinions of others

● accepting differences between oneself and others

● evaluating information

Time
15–20 minutes

Materials
• 1 activity sheet
per student

WHAT IS IT?

It's a self-assessment activity. The self-surveys can be used as unit introductions, "benchmark" assessments for ongoing study, or closure activities. Students are required to think beyond a simple "yes" or "no" response by looking for evidence of the kinds of personal behaviors that support their answers. Clarifying the relationship between what students think and what they do is an important part of building the self-awareness necessary to make healthy choices.

HOW TO DO IT

Step 1: Review the survey. Modify the statements as needed to meet the needs of your students.

Step 2: Before students begin, read the statements and clarify any directions and answer questions as needed.

Step 3: Have students complete the assessment.

Step 4: Process and provide appropriate closure for the activity.

KEY SKILLS TO BE LEARNED AND PRACTICED

● assessing personal strengths and weaknesses

● identifying personal likes and dislikes

● gathering information

● evaluating information

● identifying internal and external influences on behavior

● identifying immediate and potential dangers

● identifying future consequences of attitudes and actions

Health Skill
Assessing Personal
Health and Risks

Meaning Under Construction

Time
ongoing

Materials
• 1 activity sheet per student

WHAT IS IT?

It's a unique way to keep pace with student interest and thought during directed instruction. As you present and build lessons based on your decisions about content and learning activities, students are given the opportunity to construct their own personal meaning alongside your instruction. A variety of "quick note prompts" encourage students to record their own thoughts, questions, concerns, conclusions and curiosities about their learning. The activity honors the rich diversity of thought present at the individual level in any learning situation.

HOW TO DO IT

Step 1: Review the activity sheet. Modify as needed.

Step 2: Decide whether the activity will continue over a single lesson, a complete unit of study, or a particular period of time, such as 3 days or a week. Then decide at what intervals or points of the instruction you will introduce the opportunity for students to choose and complete the prompt that best meets their thinking and reasoning needs at that time.

(Note: Once students become familiar with the activity, they may be able to assume responsibility for their own pacing of its use.)

Step 3: Introduce and review the activity sheet directions with students.

Step 4: At the appropriate point, model the use of one of the activity prompts.

Step 5: Invite students to periodically share their responses.

Step 6: Process and provide appropriate closure for the activity.

KEY SKILLS TO BE LEARNED AND PRACTICED

● gathering, organizing and evaluating information

● recognizing the need for decisions

● analyzing complex issues

● clarifying issues of importance and personal expectations

● identifying immediate and future consequences of personal choices and behaviors

Health Skill
Making
Decisions

Anatomy of an Emotion

Time
15–20 minutes

Materials
• 1 activity sheet
  per student

WHAT IS IT?

It's a creative way to help students increase their awareness of the impact of emotions on behavior choices. Students are presented with an emotion relevant to the current unit of study. They are asked to annotate a figure with the physical, mental, emotional and social reactions that typically occur. They then explore the possible influence of these thoughts, feelings and actions on the ability to make healthy choices or to continue to pursue healthy actions in a time of challenge.

HOW TO DO IT

Step 1: Review the emotion prompt(s). Modify as needed. When topics provide you with a choice of opposite emotions, you can select one or the other, or assign a different one to each half of the class and compare results. Decide if students will post their work.

Step 2: Introduce the activity and review the example response.

Step 3: Allow students to complete and share their activity sheets.

Step 4: Discuss the impact of the emotion(s) on a behavior choice that often accompanies the given topic.

Step 5: Provide appropriate closure for the activity. Post the activity sheets if desired.

KEY SKILLS TO BE LEARNED AND PRACTICED

● recognizing and anticipating situations that cause stress

● identifying internal influences on behavior

● clarifying personal expectations

● identifying healthy coping strategies

● identifying social support systems

● making accommodations to change

● reassessing situations to alter one's perceptions of stressors

Health Skill
Managing
Stress

Time
20–30 minutes

Materials
• 1 activity sheet per student

WHAT IS IT?

It's a cooperative writing activity. Individual students are first given the opportunity to write about and explore personal knowledge and attitudes about an engaging subject related to the current topic of study. They then collaborate in small groups to compose a mini-essay that incorporates the collective thoughts and expressions of the team.

HOW TO DO IT

Step 1: Review the word prompts. Modify as needed.

Step 2: Present the activity sheet and allow students to write individually until they have a 3–5 sentence reaction.

Step 3: Group students into teams of 3–4 members. Direct the teams to collaborate to compose a mini-essay that incorporates their individual writings into a single coherent expression of the team's thoughts, feelings and attitudes about the prompt.

Step 4: Have groups share their writings.

Step 5: Process and provide appropriate closure for the activity. If desired, post the essays for future reference.

KEY SKILLS TO BE LEARNED AND PRACTICED

● initiating conversation

● expressing oneself verbally and nonverbally

● listening, processing and clarifying verbal and nonverbal communications

● responding to verbal and nonverbal requests

● accepting differences between oneself and others

● identifying and overcoming communication barriers

Health Skill
Communicating with Others

Peer View Mirror

Time
1–2 periods

Materials
• 1 activity sheet
per student

WHAT IS IT?

It's a peer interview and survey activity. The questionnaires require students to find and talk to 3 peers outside their immediate class. The survey results are tallied, analyzed and synthesized into conclusions relevant to the current unit of study. Students constantly offer the universal responses "everybody," "nobody," "always" and "never" when talking about today's key teen health issues. This activity tests assumptions about peer thinking and norms and provides "real" data for consideration.

HOW TO DO IT

Step 1: Secure approval from administration to conduct the peer survey activity. Review the survey questions and modify as needed.

Step 2: Review the survey with students before they begin.

Step 3: Review the results of the surveys as a class. Analyze the pattern of peer responses and draw conclusions to be tested during the current unit of study. Post the conclusions.

Step 4: Process and provide appropriate closure for the activity.

KEY SKILLS TO BE LEARNED AND PRACTICED

● initiating conversations

● expressing oneself verbally

● listening to, processing and clarifying verbal exchanges

● listening to new ideas and options

● accepting differences between oneself and others

Health Skill
Communicating
with Others

Time
1–2 periods, or
independent work

Materials
• 1 activity sheet
per student

WHAT IS IT?

It's a student-generated public service announcement, for peers by peers, that raises awareness, educates and delivers the "call to action" for healthy choices based on a personal quality or "virtue" related to the current topic of study.* The integration of these positive virtues into health instruction offers students the chance to name a desirable behavior and connect it to a desirable outcome.

HOW TO DO IT

Step 1: Secure approval for the campaign and the use of the school P.A. system.

Step 2: Guide students through a constructive discussion about the quality that the campaign will focus on and its relationship to the topic of study.

Step 3: Use the All Call activity sheet to direct and complete the project.

Step 4: Deliver the campaign.

Step 5: Process and evaluate the campaign. Provide appropriate closure for the activity.

KEY SKILLS TO BE LEARNED AND PRACTICED

- advocating for the health of self and others
- clarifying personal beliefs and values
- accepting differences between oneself and others
- generating ideas
- evaluating and considering options
- accessing resources
- initiating specific action

Health Skill
Negotiating
for Health

*All Call texts have been adapted from *Honesty, Perseverance and Other Virtues* by Reynold Bean (Santa Cruz, CA: ETR Associates, 1992).

The
Call
Is For
You

Time
30–45 minutes

Materials
• 1 activity sheet
per group

WHAT IS IT?

It's a problem-solving exercise. Realistic "phone calls" invite students into the thoughts, feelings and situations of young people who are "just like them." Using experience, compassion and empathy in combination with communication, decision-making, stress-management and goal-setting skills, students offer advice to these peers. The activity is a safe way to "test drive" their knowledge, attitudes and thinking skills.

HOW TO DO IT

Please note that the situations and problems portrayed in the phone calls need to be carefully reviewed before use. Modify the scenarios as needed to meet the needs of your students.

Step 1: Put students into cooperative learning groups of 3–4.

Step 2: Review the directions with students. Assign the selected call or calls. Emphasize the need to sort out the relevant facts and attitudes expressed. Guide students to identify the "real" problem at hand.

Step 3: Have groups share their scenarios and responses. Invite further discussion and insights. Proceed until all groups have presented.

Step 4: Process and provide appropriate closure for the activity.

KEY SKILLS TO BE LEARNED AND PRACTICED

● promoting clarification of personal beliefs and values

● promoting articulation of personal, family and cultural beliefs and needs

● promoting resisting of pressure from others

● promoting resolution of conflict

● promoting refuting of the arguments of others

Health Skill
Negotiating
for Health

Healthy Haiku

Time
15 minutes, plus some independent thinking time

Materials
• 1 activity sheet per student

WHAT IS IT?

It's a great way to use creative writing to focus and sharpen student thinking about a variety of health topics. Using the concise poetry form of haiku, students are invited to portray the issues, images and emotions relevant to the current topic of study. An oral reading and the posting of student work is a simple and enjoyable way to bring closure to the unit of study.

HOW TO DO IT

Step 1: Promote an oral brainstorming session around the issues, images and emotions that are or were a part of the topic of study.

Step 2: Review the format requirements of haiku and the activity sheet. Announce when and how results will be shared.

Step 3: Allow students about 10 minutes of work time and ask them to continue their work outside of class.

Step 4: Share the results of the activity and post the poems.

KEY SKILLS TO BE LEARNED AND PRACTICED

- assessing personal likes and dislikes
- articulating preferences
- clarifying issues of importance to oneself and others
- identifying opportunities to reward healthy choices and behaviors
- validating a personal sense of reality

Health Skill
Rewarding
Healthy Behavior

for Health

Time
20–30 minutes

Materials
• 1 activity sheet per student

WHAT IS IT?

It's an opportunity for students to advocate for the healthful well-being of themselves and others. As they generate a list of tips and suggestions to improve personal health attitudes and actions, they will demonstrate their ability to apply health content to real-life choices and behaviors. Posting the lists in hallways, libraries and other student centers is a great way to spread a "healthy word" to other peers and adults alike.

HOW TO DO IT

Step 1: Review the activity sheet. Modify as needed.

Step 2: Review the activity directions and guide a discussion about the kinds of tips or advice that might be included on students' lists.

Step 3: Have students complete the activity.

Step 4: Post the lists in locations where peers and adults will benefit from your students' healthy advice.

KEY SKILLS TO BE LEARNED AND PRACTICED

Health Skill
Negotiating
for Health

● modeling and promoting clarification of personal beliefs and values

● modeling and promoting articulation of personal needs

● modeling and promoting resisting of pressure from others

● modeling and promoting openness to new ideas and options

● modeling and promoting personal choices and actions for healthful well-being

Steps Toward My Future

WHAT IS IT?

It's a quick, simple, visual activity that helps students focus their learning and thinking on a future health goal related to the unit of study. Students identify the resources, attitudes, skills, knowledge, actions and steps that will help them maintain or reach an identified health goal. The exercise helps fortify the personal knowledge and intentions that eventually translate into healthy behaviors.

HOW TO DO IT

Step 1: Introduce the activity as an opportunity for students to organize their thinking and learning into a "big picture" look at using what they know to stay or be healthy.

Step 2: Review the topic and stated goal on the first page of the activity sheet. Allow students time to list various resources to complete the first part of the activity.

Step 3: Have students begin the next part of the activity by completing the prompts on the second page of the activity sheet. Invite them to share their work with each other.

Step 4: Have students revisit their work, make desired modifications and finalize their statements. Suggest that they post the completed activity sheets in a place where they will be reminded of their health goal and what they must do to realize it.

KEY SKILLS TO BE LEARNED AND PRACTICED

- assessing needs, strengths and weaknesses
- assessing availability of resources
- clarifying personal expectations
- projecting future scenarios
- identifying possible consequences of future actions
- reducing complex steps to simple components
- initiating specific action

Health Skill
Setting and
Achieving Goals

Abstinence

Thinking and Talking About Abstinence

ASK, LISTEN AND LEARN

Use 1 of the following questions as a **Question Roll Call** prompt (modify if needed). Write the selected question on the board and ask students to think about a response. Call roll. Students use their answer to the question to replace the traditional response of "here" or "present."

1. What percentage of kids your age do you believe are sexually abstinent?

2. What are some popular reasons not to have sex?

3. Where does the most pressure to be sexually active come from?

4. Do you think music videos promote sex for young people? Why or why not?

5. What kind of reputation does virginity have?

The Choice to Abstain

READ, THINK AND DISCUSS

I stand in front of the mirror...

Imagining how *you* see me...Do you *really* see *me*?

Getting ready...Hair in place, just the right clothes, smelling nice.

Thinking about us...kisses, hugs and holding hands.

Warm, achy feelings inside...just like you. Or is it like you?

You...Pushing so hard to do something about it...

And the pressure of those words you say to me—

"What's wrong with you? It's what people do to prove their love."

Is it?

Is that the only way to show it?

CONSTRUCT YOUR OWN MEANING

As a class, discuss the reading by first sharing your initial reactions. Then identify the issues involved in this situation.

Signs of the Times

Virginity

COMPLETE AND POST IT

Carefully read and complete the sign by filling in what you think are some of the attitudes, practices or beliefs that have followed the subject of virginity through time. Post your work as directed.

_____ believes...
YOUR NAME

In the past, virginity was
_____
_____
_____
_____

Today, virginity is
_____
_____
_____
_____
_____

In the future,
virginity will probably be
_____
_____
_____

Abstinence

Thinking About Saying No to Sex

COLLABORATE AND CREATE

As a group, discuss your reactions to and the issues you identify with saying no to sex. Use the letters of the words creatively to record the key points of your discussion. You might want to work out a rough draft first. Be prepared to post your work and share it with the class.

S _____

A _____

Y _____

I _____

N _____

G _____

N _____

O _____

T _____

O _____

S _____

E _____

X _____

Abstinence

Me and Abstinence

READ AND RESPOND

Read the statements and select a "yes" or "no" response for each. Use the last column to describe evidence of your own personal behavior that supports your answer.

Statements	Yes or No?	My Evidence
1. I respect sexual abstinence as a positive choice.		
2. I know the advantages of sexual abstinence.		
3. I agree that my sexuality is only one part of who I am.		
4. I am aware of healthy ways to express affection without sex.		
5. I can resist pressure from others.		

REVIEW AND RESPOND

Review your responses and evidence. Use the back of this sheet to write at least 7 sentences about the profile of you they reveal. Say what you think or feel about this profile and what impact it has on your health and well-being today as well as in the future.

Think, Choose, Act Healthy

Exploring My Thinking About Abstinence

Abstinence

THINK, SELECT AND RESPOND

Use this sheet during your lesson(s) about abstinence. At the teacher's signal, select and complete the prompt that best fits your personal thinking at the time. Be prepared to share your thoughts with others.

In my opinion, abstinence is...
_____
_____
_____
_____
_____

But what if...
_____
_____
_____
_____

I'm beginning to change the way I...
_____
_____
_____
_____
_____

It surprised me that...
_____
_____
_____
_____

I think teens who choose abstinence are...
_____
_____
_____
_____
_____

I think teens who choose to be sexually active are...
_____
_____
_____
_____

The bottom line for me is that abstinence is...
_____
_____
_____

Think, Choose, Act Healthy

© ETR Associates

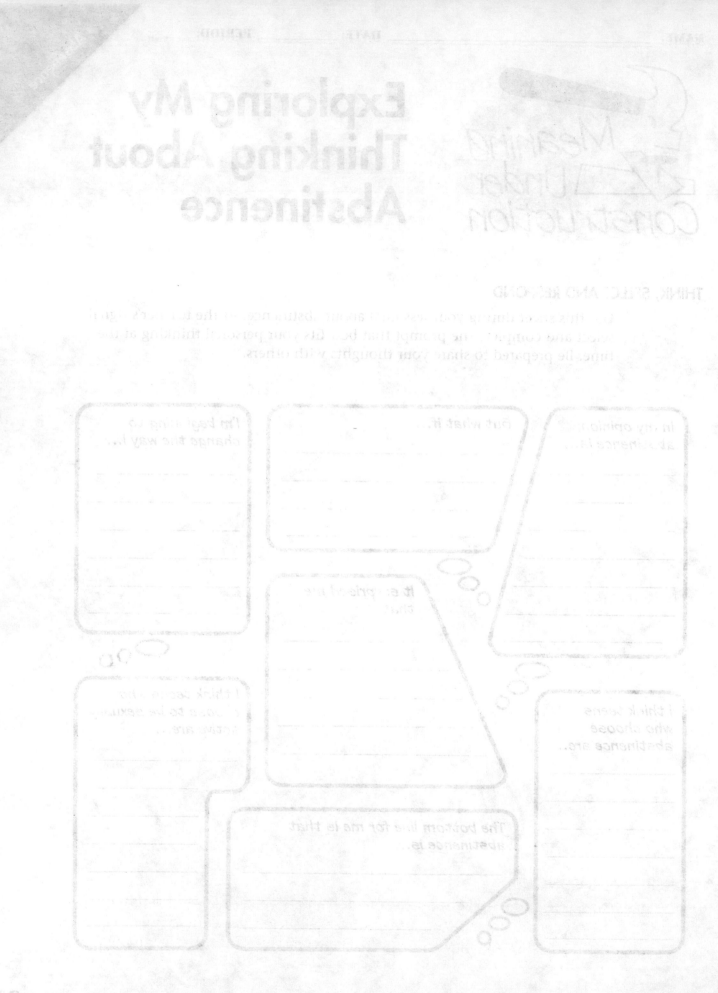

Love and Abstinence

THINK AND ANNOTATE

Take a few moments to think about love. Annotate the figure to show what this emotion can make a person think, say and do. A sample has been done for you.

You think about the person all the time.

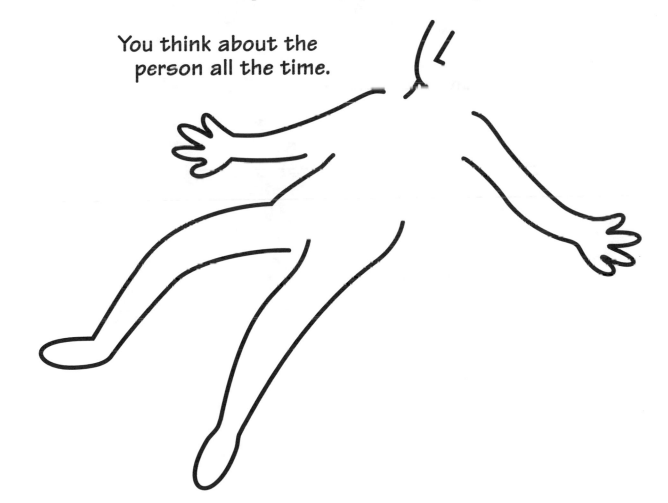

CONSIDER AND CONCLUDE

State what impact you think love has on a person's attitude and ability to make healthy choices about abstaining from sexual activity. Identify some people and personal actions that could help a person cope with this powerful emotion in a healthy way.

Passion

THINK AND WRITE

Think about how the following word, idea or image relates to the topic of abstinence. Write down your thoughts until you have a reaction that is at least 3–5 sentences long.

_____

_____

_____

_____

_____

_____

_____

_____

_____

_____

COLLABORATE AND WRITE ABOUT IT AGAIN

As a team, begin by sharing your individual responses. Then, using a new sheet of paper and your original writings, compose a single mini-essay that represents the team thoughts, feelings and attitudes about the word or phrase. Be prepared to share your work with the class.

REVIEW AND PROCESS

Discuss your team's essay. Talk about your points of agreement and differences of opinion. What kinds of resolutions does your group essay reflect?

Sexual Reputation

THINK AND WRITE

Think about how the following phrase, idea or image relates to the topic of abstinence. Write down your thoughts until you have a reaction that is at least 3–5 sentences long.

_____

_____

_____

_____

_____

_____

_____

_____

_____

COLLABORATE AND WRITE ABOUT IT AGAIN

As a team, begin by sharing your individual responses. Then, using a new sheet of paper and your original writings, compose a single mini-essay that represents the team thoughts, feelings and attitudes about the word or phrase. Be prepared to share your work with the class.

REVIEW AND PROCESS

Discuss your team's essay. Talk about your points of agreement and differences of opinion. What kinds of resolutions does your group essay reflect?

Peer View Mirror

Choices About Sex and Me

SURVEY YOUR PEERS

Use the following questions to interview 3 of your friends or peers on the topic of sex. Use the back of this sheet to record the responses. Use the steps at the bottom of this sheet to tally and discuss your survey results.

SURVEY QUESTIONS

1. What do you think is the most serious consequence of early sexual activity?

2. How much attention do people pay to sexual reputations?

3. How true is the statement that "everybody is doing it"?

ANALYZE AND CONCLUDE

1. As a class, tally the results of your survey questions on the board.

2. Examine the results and discuss any obvious trends, patterns or unexpected responses.

3. For each question, formulate a conclusion based on the responses. Post the conclusions in a visible spot to refer to during this unit of study.

Being Prudent and Choosing Abstinence

Abstinence

YOUR CHALLENGE

Use what you know and are learning about abstinence to tell your peers how being prudent can help people choose to abstain from sexual activity.

THINK ABOUT IT

- Being prudent is about using sound and cautious judgment. Prudent people act in a careful manner.
- Prudence is a personal virtue that is often considered "old fashioned."
- Decisions made based on being prudent support future goals and plans.

DESIGN AND DELIVER

Using the Challenge and Think About It statements, design and deliver a P.A. system campaign to educate and motivate your peers to call upon personal prudence to abstain from sexual activity.

PROJECT STEPS

1. Work as a class to brainstorm a list of the kinds of ideas, themes and basic information that would help your peers and friends recognize and value the role being prudent plays in choosing to abstain from sexual activity.

2. Work as collaborative groups to design at least 3 appropriate messages that could be part of a week-long P.A. campaign.

3. As a class, select the best messages and some announcers for the campaign.

4. Practice with the P.A. system after school.

5. Deliver and evaluate the effectiveness of the campaign.

Abstinence

Respecting the Commitment to Abstain

COLLABORATE AND ADVISE

As a group, take the phone call of a peer in need of help and advice. Work to problem-solve the scenario assigned to your group. Put yourself in the caller's place. Offer the healthiest advice you can. Be ready to share and discuss your responses with the class.

Caller #1

We're Not Really in Control...

She's my first girlfriend—my first everything, from kisses to hugs. We've talked about how we want to show our affection, and we've chosen not to have sex right now. We both have things we want to do in our lives and sex would complicate things. But we've started to party with some friends who drink. The alcohol really makes it hard for us to be around each other and still be in control. She says she can handle it, and that I can too if I just lighten up and relax. But I don't want to make any mistakes I can't take back. What can I do?

Continued

Caller #1

We're Not Really in Control...

Respecting the Commitment to Abstain

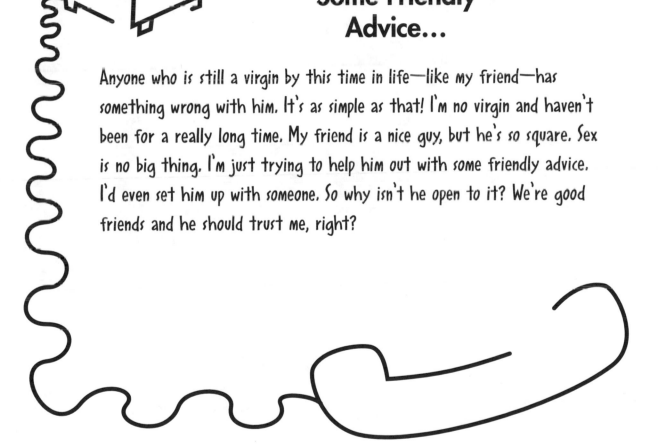

Caller #2

Some Friendly Advice...

Anyone who is still a virgin by this time in life—like my friend—has something wrong with him. It's as simple as that! I'm no virgin and haven't been for a really long time. My friend is a nice guy, but he's so square. Sex is no big thing. I'm just trying to help him out with some friendly advice. I'd even set him up with someone. So why isn't he open to it? We're good friends and he should trust me, right?

Respecting Myself

THINK, FOCUS AND EXPRESS

Using haiku format, compose a poem about respecting yourself. Present the issues, images or emotions that you think are a part of this challenge. Use the form below to help you write your haiku. Be ready to read and post your work.

Haiku

Five short syl-la-bles,
then fol-low with sev-en more.
Five a-gain, the end.

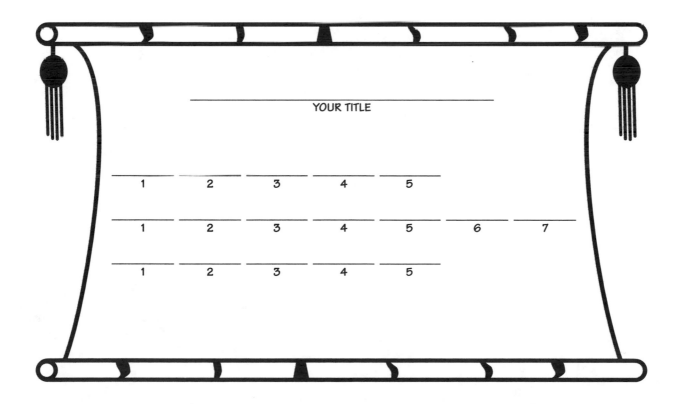

YOUR TITLE

	1	2	3	4	5		

| | 1 | 2 | 3 | 4 | 5 | 6 | 7 |

| | 1 | 2 | 3 | 4 | 5 | | |

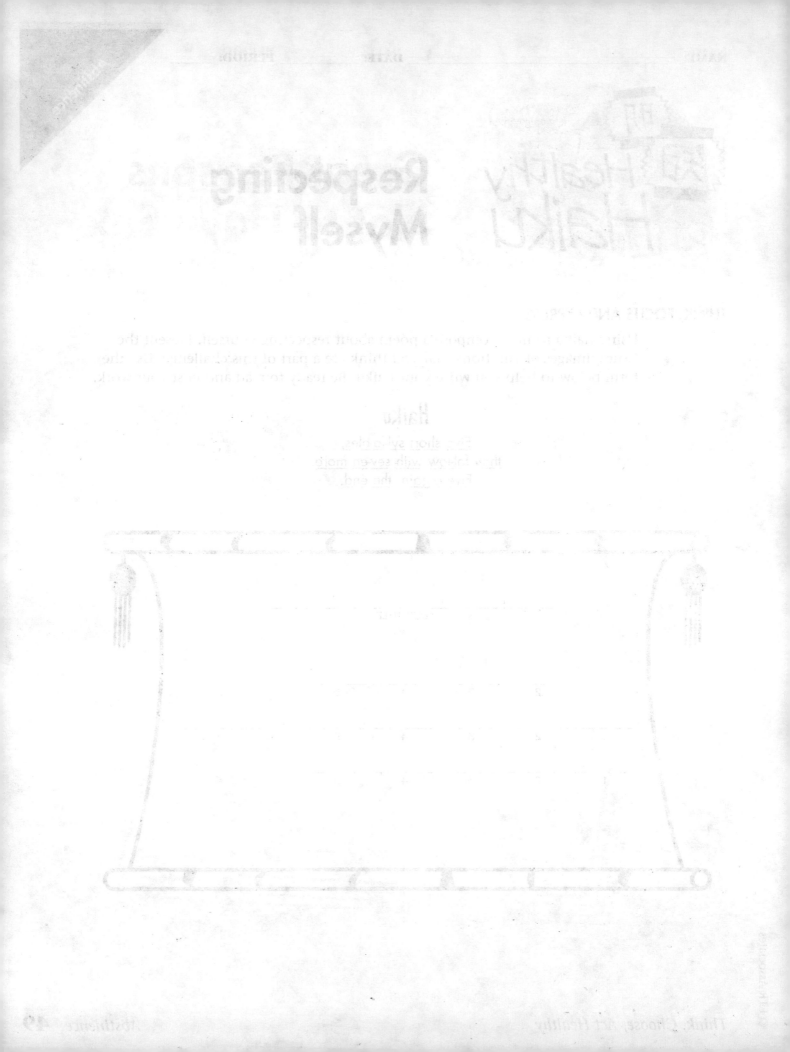

Great Reasons Not to Have Sex

THINK AND PRESCRIBE

Consider all you know about abstinence. Generate a list of persuasive reasons for young people to commit to abstaining from sex.

Rx PEER CLINIC

10 Great Reasons Not to Have Sex

1. _____
2. _____
3. _____
4. _____
5. _____
6. _____
7. _____
8. _____
9. _____
10. _____

Dr. _____
　　　　　　YOUR NAME

Think, Choose, Act Healthy

Steps Toward My Future

Being Sexually Abstinent

CONSIDER, GENERATE AND APPLY

Think about the healthy goal in the center of the activity sheet. List as many resources and behaviors as you can think of that will help you build your path toward this goal. Use this information to complete the "steps" on the next page. Share and discuss your work. Finalize your responses and post your activity sheet as directed.

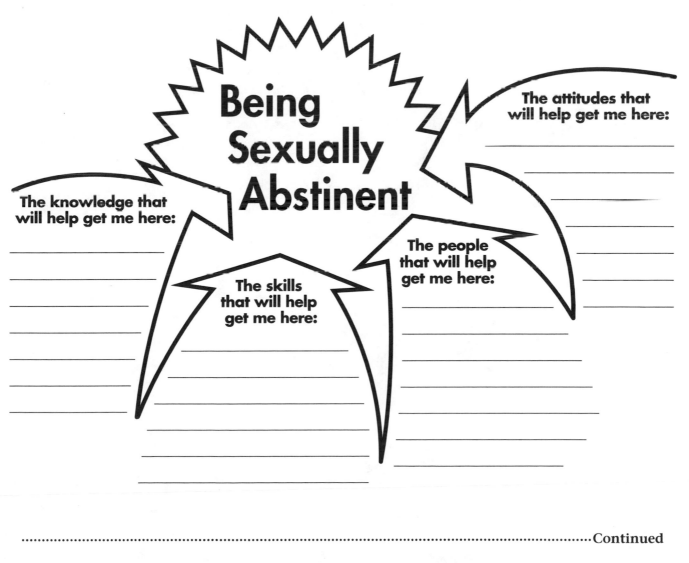

Being Sexually Abstinent

The attitudes that will help get me here:
_____
_____
_____
_____

The knowledge that will help get me here:
_____
_____
_____
_____

The people that will help get me here:
_____
_____
_____
_____

The skills that will help get me here:
_____
_____
_____
_____

Continued

Steps
Toward
My
Future

A Skill that I will work on is

because…

It will be important to remember…

When I need help, I will talk with

because…

If I have to, I will even…

For me, the consequences of not being sexually abstinent could be...

Body Image and Eating Disorders

Thinking and Talking About Bodies and Nutrition

ASK, LISTEN AND LEARN

Use 1 of the following questions as a **Question Roll Call** prompt (modify if needed). Write the selected question on the board and ask students to think about a response. Call roll. Students use their answer to the question to replace the traditional response of "here" or "present."

Body Image

1. Where does the most pressure to have the perfect body come from?

2. Is the pressure to look good the same for boys and girls?

3. What effects can TV advertising have on a person's self-image?

4. What happens when people judge others on the basis of body image?

5. What kinds of risks will teens take to have the perfect body?

Nutrition

6. What did you have for breakfast today?

7. What is the healthiest food a person can eat?

8. How many glasses of water a day do you drink?

9. What are your favorite snack foods?

10. What is the healthiest food you know how to cook or prepare?

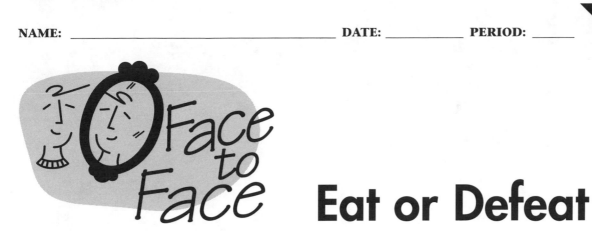

Eat or Defeat

READ, THINK AND DISCUSS

Fast food breakfasts, sodas, jelly donuts.

Empty food bags stuffed under the car seat...

A 2-mile run.

"I'm not hungry. Fruit and a diet soda will do."

From the vending machine—potato chips, candy bars and cookies.

Wrappers stashed in a locker...

"Cottage cheese, please. But not too much."

Hours in the weight room.

At the mall—a pizza, french fries, a cinnamon roll and a Coke.

"Just vegetables. No, I'm not sick. I'm just not hungry."

Alone at night, 150 sit-ups.

A drawer full of food hidden away...

Feelings of disgust and defeat...

CONSTRUCT YOUR OWN MEANING

As a class, discuss the reading by first sharing your initial reactions. Then identify the issues involved in this situation.

Body Image

Being Beautiful or Handsome

COMPLETE AND POST IT

Carefully read and complete the sign by filling in what you think are some of the attitudes, practices or beliefs that have followed the subject of being beautiful or handsome through time. Post your work as directed.

_____ believes...
YOUR NAME

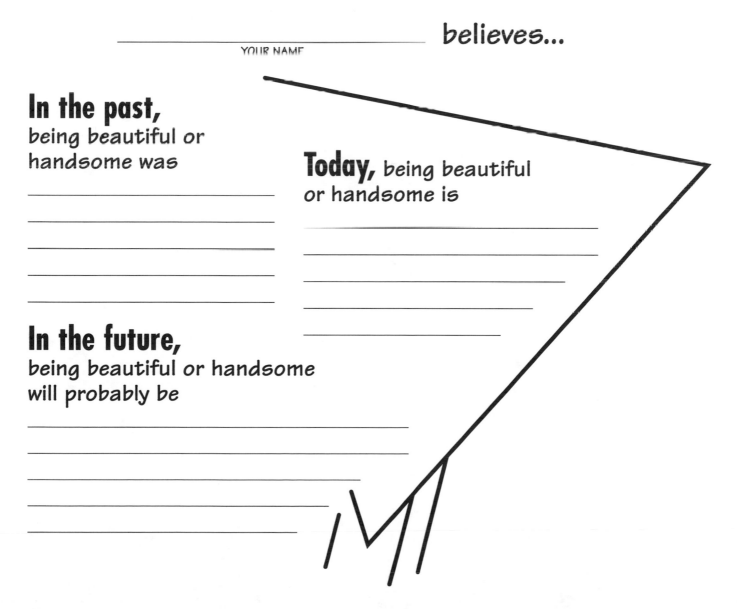

In the past, being beautiful or handsome was

_____
_____
_____
_____

Today, being beautiful or handsome is

_____
_____
_____
_____

In the future, being beautiful or handsome will probably be

_____
_____
_____
_____

Body Image

Thinking About Models

COLLABORATE AND CREATE

As a group, discuss your reactions to and the issues you identify with models in the media. Use the letters of the words creatively to record the key points of your discussion. You might want to work out a rough draft first. Be prepared to post your work and share it with the class.

M _____

O _____

D _____

E _____

L _____

S _____

Thinking About Junk Food

COLLABORATE AND CREATE

As a group, discuss your reactions to and the issues you identify with junk food. Use the letters of the words creatively to record the key points of your discussion. You might want to work out a rough draft first. Be prepared to post your work and share it with the class.

J _____

U _____

N _____

K _____

F _____

O _____

O _____

D _____

Me and Body Image

Body Image

READ AND RESPOND

Read the statements and select a "yes" or "no" response for each. Use the last column to describe evidence of your own personal behavior that supports your answer.

Statements	Yes or No?	My Evidence
1. I feel comfortable about my physical image.		
2. I can list my best physical features.		
3. I realize that I am more than my physical appearance.		
4. I can put the bodies of models in proper perspective.		
5. I don't judge others based on their physical appearance.		

REVIEW AND RESPOND

Review your responses and evidence. Use the back of this sheet to write at least 7 sentences about the profile of you they reveal. Say what you think or feel about this profile and what impact it has on your health and well-being today as well as in the future.

Think, Choose, Act Healthy

Me and Nutrition

READ AND RESPOND

Read the statements and select a "yes" or "no" response for each.
Use the last column to describe evidence of your own personal behavior that supports your answer.

Statements	Yes or No?	My Evidence
1. I eat a healthy breakfast regularly.		
2. I eat a variety of foods daily.		
3. I choose to eat foods that are low in fat.		
4. I drink at least 8 glasses of water a day.		
5. I am aware of how my diet affects my health.		

REVIEW AND RESPOND

Review your responses and evidence. Use the back of this sheet to write at least 7 sentences about the profile of you they reveal. Say what you think or feel about this profile and what impact it has on your health and well-being today as well as in the future.

Think, Choose, Act Healthy

Meaning Under Construction

Exploring My Thinking About Body Image

Body Image

THINK, SELECT AND RESPOND

Use this sheet during your lesson(s) about body image. At the teacher's signal, select and complete the prompt that best fits your personal thinking at the time. Be prepared to share your thoughts with others.

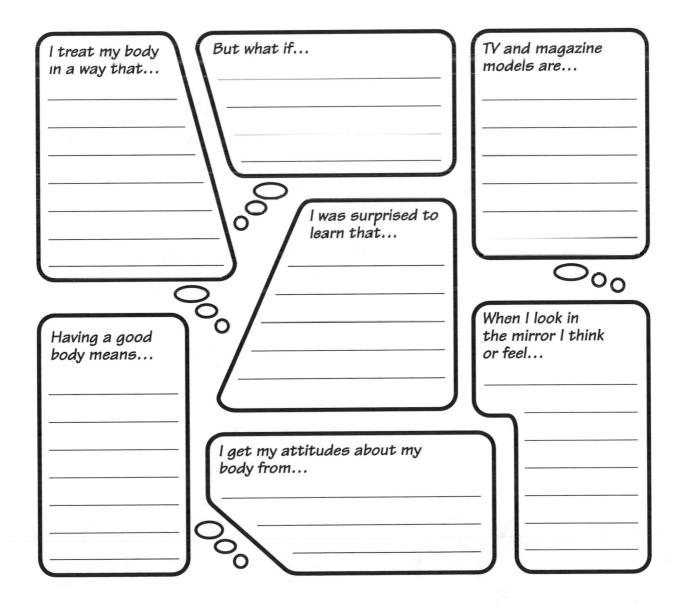

I treat my body in a way that...

But what if...

TV and magazine models are...

I was surprised to learn that...

Having a good body means...

When I look in the mirror I think or feel...

I get my attitudes about my body from...

Exploring My Thinking About Nutrition and Eating Disorders

THINK, SELECT AND RESPOND

Use this sheet during your lesson(s) about nutrition or eating disorders. At the teacher's signal, select and complete the prompt that best fits your personal thinking at the time. Be prepared to share your thoughts with others.

My relationship with food is...
_____
_____
_____
_____
_____
_____

I think the diet I eat...
_____
_____
_____
_____

My favorite food is...
_____
_____
_____
_____
_____

Eating disorders and guys...
_____
_____
_____
_____
_____

I was surprised to hear others say that...
_____
_____
_____
_____
_____

The way I eat now will affect my future by...
_____
_____
_____

I think a person gets an eating disorder because...
_____
_____
_____
_____

Think, Choose, Act Healthy

Shame and Body Image

THINK AND ANNOTATE

Take a few moments to think about shame. Annotate the figure to show what this emotion can make a person think, say and do. A sample has been done for you.

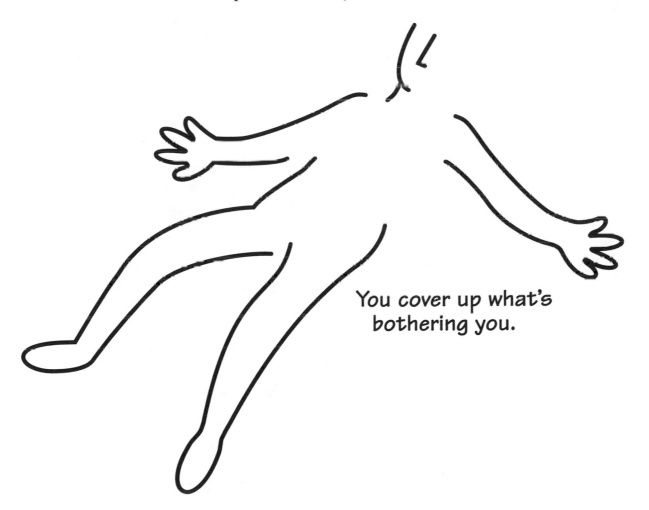

You cover up what's bothering you.

CONSIDER AND CONCLUDE

State what impact you think shame has on a person's attitude and ability to resist taking radical risks to change his or her physical appearance. Identify some people and personal actions that could help a person cope with this emotion in a healthy way.

Think, Choose, Act Healthy

Pride and Body Image

THINK AND ANNOTATE

Take a few moments to think about pride. Annotate the figure to show what this emotion can make a person think, say and do. A sample has been done for you.

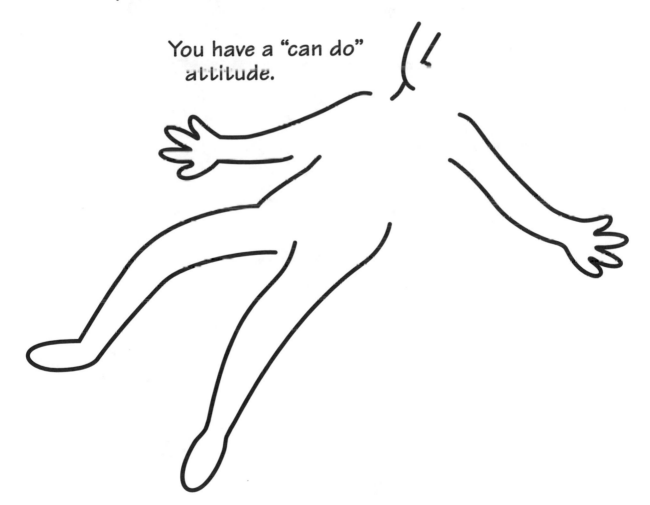

You have a "can do" attitude.

CONSIDER AND CONCLUDE

State what impact you think pride has on a person's attitude and ability to make healthy changes in his or her physical appearance. Identify some people and personal actions that could help a person maintain this healthy emotion.

Think, Choose, Act Healthy

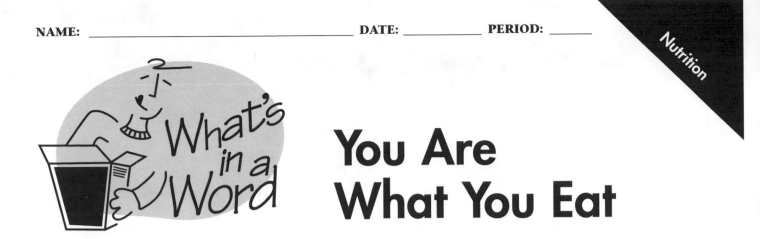

You Are What You Eat

THINK AND WRITE

Think about how the following phrase, idea or image relates to the topic of nutrition. Write down your thoughts until you have a reaction that is at least 3–5 sentences long.

You Are What You Eat

_____
_____
_____
_____
_____
_____
_____
_____
_____
_____

COLLABORATE AND WRITE ABOUT IT AGAIN

As a team, begin by sharing your individual responses. Then, using a new sheet of paper and your original writings, compose a single mini-essay that represents the team thoughts, feelings and attitudes about the word or phrase. Be prepared to share your work with the class.

REVIEW AND PROCESS

Discuss your team's essay. Talk about your points of agreement and differences of opinion. What kinds of resolutions does your group essay reflect?

Bulimia, Anorexia and Me

SURVEY YOUR PEERS

Use the following questions to interview 3 of your friends or peers on the topic of eating disorders. Use the back of this sheet to record the responses. Use the steps at the bottom of this sheet to tally and discuss your survey results.

SURVEY QUESTIONS

1. How real are bulimia and anorexia among the teens you know?

2. What pressures push a person to risk this kind of behavior?

3. Why do you think girls are more often affected by eating disorders than boys?

ANALYZE AND CONCLUDE

1. As a class, tally the results of your survey questions on the board.

2. Examine the results and discuss any obvious trends, patterns or unexpected responses.

3. For each question, formulate a conclusion based on the responses. Post the conclusions in a visible spot to refer to during this unit of study.

Food Choices and Me

SURVEY YOUR PEERS

Use the following questions to interview 3 of your friends or peers on the topic of nutrition. Use the back of this sheet to record the responses. Use the steps at the bottom of this sheet to tally and discuss your survey results.

SURVEY QUESTIONS

1. Do you think much about your eating habits?

2. Do you eat a reasonably nutritious diet?

3. How often in a day do you drink water?

ANALYZE AND CONCLUDE

1. As a class, tally the results of your survey questions on the board.

2. Examine the results and discuss any obvious trends, patterns or unexpected responses.

3. For each question, formulate a conclusion based on the responses. Post the conclusions in a visible spot to refer to during this unit of study.

Being Compassionate and Respecting Body Image

YOUR CHALLENGE

Use what you know and are learning about body image to tell your peers how being compassionate can help a person maintain a healthy attitude about body image.

THINK ABOUT IT

- It requires a great deal of compassion to accept and value differences in body image or overall physical appearance.

- Being compassionate is about being aware and experiencing understanding. It may or may not be connected to taking action.

- A key experience of being compassionate is to imagine yourself in the other person's place.

DESIGN AND DELIVER

Using the Challenge and Think About It statements, design and deliver a P.A. system campaign to educate and motivate your peers to maintain a healthy view of diverse body images.

PROJECT STEPS

1. Work as a class to brainstorm a list of the kinds of ideas, themes and basic information that would help your peers and friends recognize and value the role being compassionate plays in maintaining a healthy view of body image.

2. Work as collaborative groups to design at least 3 appropriate messages that could be part of a week-long P.A. campaign.

3. As a class, select the best messages and some announcers for the campaign.

4. Practice with the P.A. system after school.

5. Deliver and evaluate the effectiveness of the campaign.

Images in the Media

COLLABORATE AND ADVISE

As a group, take the phone call of a peer in need of help and advice. Work to problem-solve the scenario assigned to your group. Put yourself in the caller's place. Offer the healthiest advice you can. Be ready to share and discuss your responses with the class.

Caller #1

Listen Up, Guys...

It's a joke to think that I could ever look like the women you see in magazine ads. I know how much make-up and photo touch-up it takes to get them to look so good. And you hear stories every day about models who starve themselves to stay thin. The problem is, I don't think guys realize this. My boyfriend is always pointing to some picture in a magazine and suggesting that I try to look the same way. Does he think I'm flattered that he wants me to look like someone else? It's really starting to get on my nerves. What can I say to make him understand how I feel?

Continued

Images in the Media

Caller #2

Listen Up, Girls...

I bet most girls don't think much about how magazine ads affect guys. I'd do anything to have the clear skin, muscles, wavy hair and perfect teeth that male models have. I see the girls swoon over the photos of all those guys with perfect bodies and fine clothes. Gimme a break! I'll never measure up. I'm just me! How do we get them to understand that we guys feel the pressure too?

Think, Choose, Act Healthy

Nutrition

The Call Is For You

Healthy Food Choices

COLLABORATE AND ADVISE

As a group, take the phone call of a peer in need of help and advice. Work to problem-solve the scenario assigned to your group. Put yourself in the caller's place. Offer the healthiest advice you can. Be ready to share and discuss your responses with the class.

Caller #1

May I Have Your Order Please?

Eating lunch at the school cafeteria and out of the vending machines is a real challenge. I usually either eat a tray full of food that leaves me feeling stuffed, or just pick at my food and go hungry the rest of the day. Does this happen to you too? How do you manage to make healthy food choices at school?

Continued

Healthy
Food Choices

Caller #2

3 Days and
10 Pounds...

Team tryouts are in 3 days, and I need to lose 10 pounds fast! All I want is to lighten up so that I can perform better on tryout day. I figure I can drink that "diet in a can stuff" for a few days, stay off real food, and limit the amount of water I drink. That should do the trick. What do you think?

Body Image

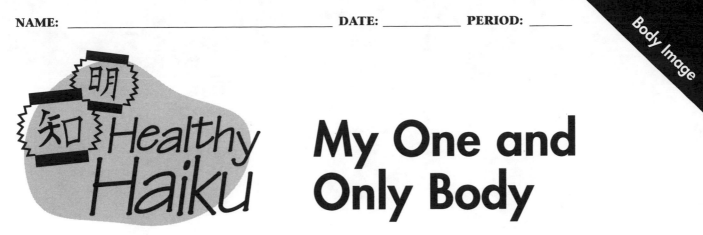

Healthy Haiku

My One and Only Body

THINK FOCUS AND EXPRESS

Using haiku format, compose a poem about your one and only body. Present the issues, images or emotions that you think are a part of this challenge. Use the form below to help you write your haiku. Be ready to read and post your work.

Haiku

Five short syl-la-bles,
then fol-low with sev-en more.
Five a-gain, the end.

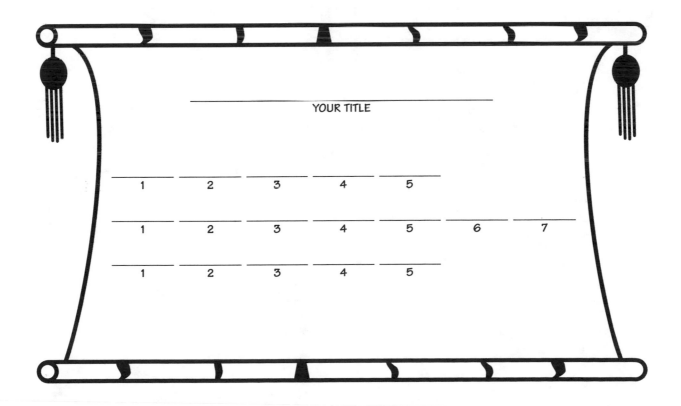

YOUR TITLE

1   2   3   4   5

1   2   3   4   5   6   7

1   2   3   4   5

Eating Healthy

THINK FOCUS AND EXPRESS

Using haiku format, compose a poem about eating healthy. Present the issues, images or emotions that you think are a part of this challenge. Use the form below to help you write your haiku. Be ready to read and post your work.

Haiku

Five short syl-la-bles,
then fol-low with sev-en more.
Five a-gain, the end.

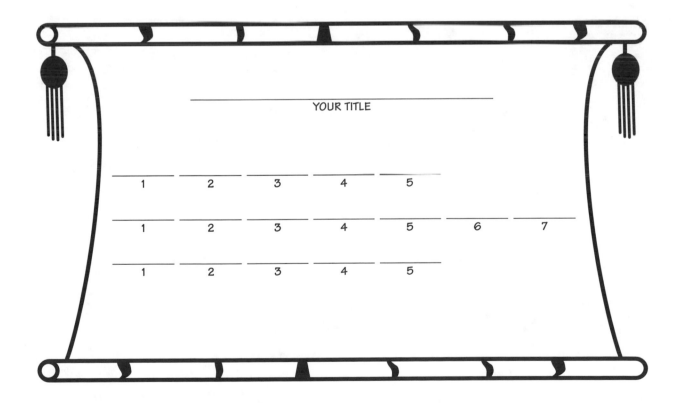

YOUR TITLE

1   2   3   4   5

1   2   3   4   5   6   7

1   2   3   4   5

Nutrition

How to Eat Healthy

THINK AND PRESCRIBE

Consider all you know about the importance of making healthy food choices on a daily basis. Generate a list of tips and advice for people to follow to eat healthy.

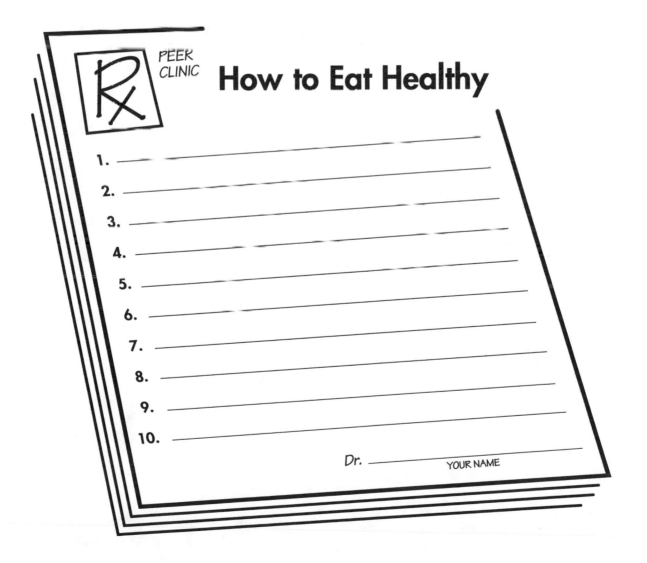

PEER CLINIC

How to Eat Healthy

1. _____
2. _____
3. _____
4. _____
5. _____
6. _____
7. _____
8. _____
9. _____
10. _____

Dr. _____ YOUR NAME

Accepting and Respecting My Body

CONSIDER, GENERATE AND APPLY

Think about the healthy goal in the center of the activity sheet. List as many resources and behaviors as you can think of that will help you build your path toward this goal. Use this information to complete the "steps" on the next page. Share and discuss your work. Finalize your responses and post your activity sheet as directed.

Accepting and Respecting My Body

The attitudes that will help get me here:

The knowledge that will help get me here:

The people that will help get me here:

The skills that will help get me here:

···Continued

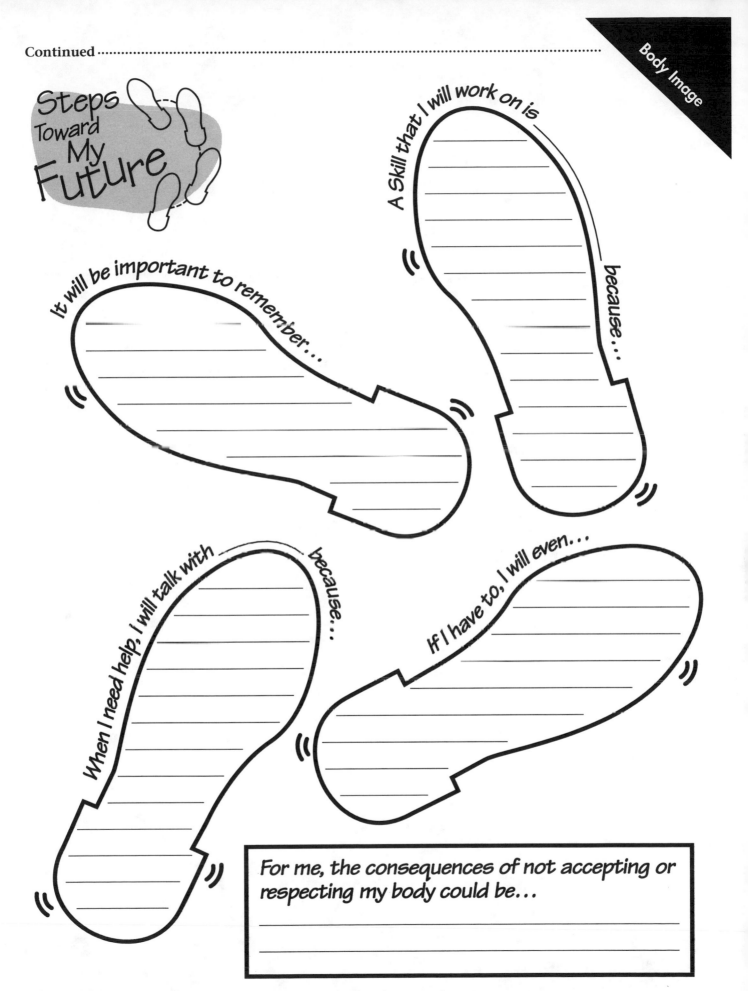

Steps Toward My Future

A Skill that I will work on is

because...

It will be important to remember...

When I need help, I will talk with

because...

If I have to, I will even...

For me, the consequences of not accepting or respecting my body could be...

Communication and Self-Esteem

Thinking and Talking About You

ASK, LISTEN AND LEARN

Use 1 of the following questions as a **Question Roll Call** prompt (modify if needed). Write the selected question on the board and ask students to think about a response. Call roll. Students use their answer to the question to replace the traditional response of "here" or "present."

1. Who are you?

2. How do others see you?

3. What do you believe?

4. What do you give to others?

5. What will you become?

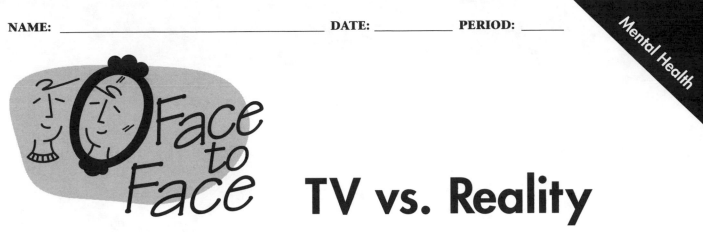

TV vs. Reality

READ, THINK AND DISCUSS

Channel 9—
   Perfect bodies, perfect houses, g-r-r-reat cars!
   Liquids, pastes and powders that swish, brush and flush your
   world clean...
Channel 5—
   Families and loyal friends, living in 30-minute worlds...
Channel 13—
   Real people, real drama, real anguish...Direct from the scene...
   "Parental discretion is advised."
MTV—
   Ooooo Baby-Baby-Ba-by Ooooo...
   "Get Smart About Sex, Drugs and AIDS!"
The 10:00 News—
   "Experts expressed concern today that many people,
   compelled by the experience of watching television,
   are now using their viewing to replace actual living."

CONSTRUCT YOUR OWN MEANING

As a class, discuss the reading by first sharing your initial reactions. Then identify the issues involved in this situation.

Signs of the Times

Coping

COMPLETE AND POST IT

Carefully read and complete the sign by filling in what you think are some of the attitudes, practices or beliefs that have followed the subject of coping through time. Post your work as directed.

_____ **believes...**
YOUR NAME

In the past, coping was
_____
_____
_____
_____

Today, coping is
_____
_____
_____
_____
_____

In the future,
coping will probably be
_____
_____
_____

Thinking About Put-Downs

COLLABORATE AND CREATE

As a group, discuss your reactions to and the issues you identify with put-downs. Use the letters of the words creatively to record the key points of your discussion. You might want to work out a rough draft first. Be prepared to post your work and share it with the class.

P _____

U _____

T _____

-

D _____

O _____

W _____

N _____

S _____

Mental Health

Me and Coping

READ AND RESPOND

Read the statements and select a "yes" or "no" response for each. Use the last column to describe evidence of your own personal behavior that supports your answer.

Statements	Yes or No?	My Evidence
1. I plan my time and work to avoid stress.		
2. I have healthy ways to relax.		
3. I relax on a regular basis.		
4. I recognize when I need help from others.		
5. I have people who can talk things out with me.		

REVIEW AND RESPOND

Review your responses and evidence. Use the back of this sheet to write at least 7 sentences about the profile of you they reveal. Say what you think or feel about this profile and what impact it has on your health and well-being today as well as in the future.

Meaning Under Construction

Exploring My Thinking About Mental Health

THINK, SELECT AND RESPOND

Use this sheet during your lesson(s) about mental health. At the teacher's signal, select and complete the prompt that best fits your personal thinking at the time. Be prepared to share your thoughts with others.

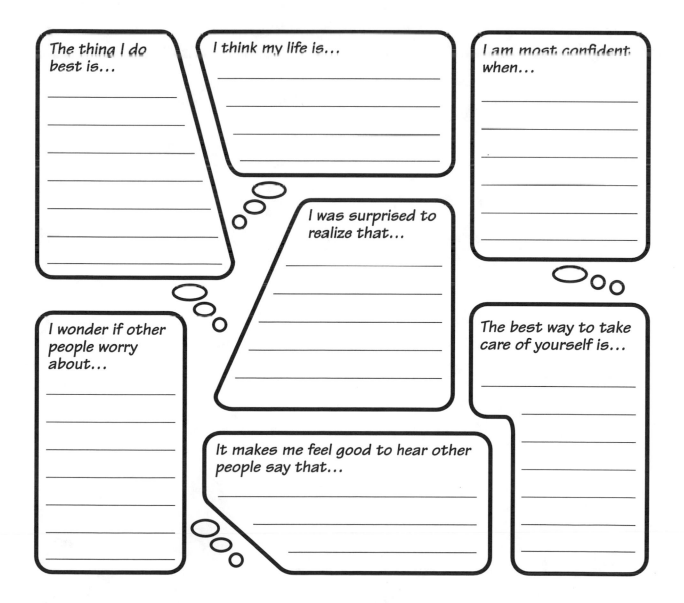

The thing I do best is...

I think my life is...

I am most confident when...

I was surprised to realize that...

I wonder if other people worry about...

The best way to take care of yourself is...

It makes me feel good to hear other people say that...

Hope and Mental Health

THINK AND ANNOTATE

Take a few moments to think about hope. Annotate the figure to show what this emotion can make a person think, say and do. A sample has been done for you.

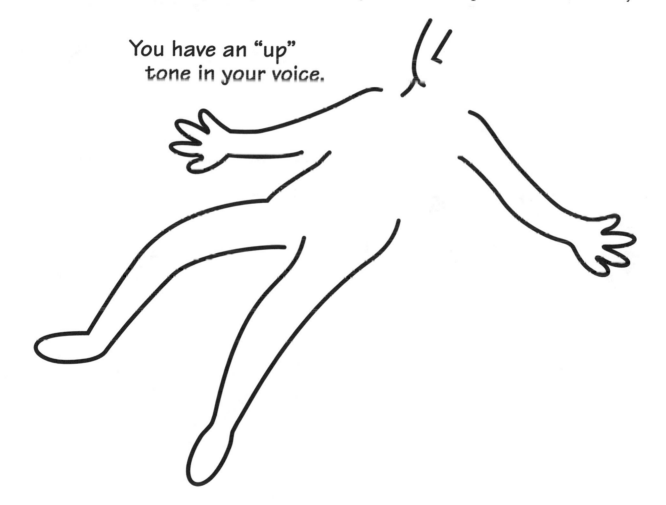

You have an "up" tone in your voice.

CONSIDER AND CONCLUDE

State what impact you think hope has on a person's attitude and ability to find healthy ways to cope with feelings of being down or helpless. Identify some people and personal actions that could help a person maintain this healthy emotion.

Giving My Best

THINK AND WRITE

Think about how the following phrase, idea or image relates to the topic of mental health. Write down your thoughts until you have a reaction that is at least 3–5 sentences long.

_____
_____
_____
_____
_____
_____
_____
_____
_____
_____

COLLABORATE AND WRITE ABOUT IT AGAIN

As a team, begin by sharing your individual responses. Then, using a new sheet of paper and your original writings, compose a single mini-essay that represents the team thoughts, feelings and attitudes about the word or phrase. Be prepared to share your work with the class.

REVIEW AND PROCESS

Discuss your team's essay. Talk about your points of agreement and differences of opinion. What kinds of resolutions does your group essay reflect?

Feeling Depressed

THINK AND WRITE

Think about how the following phrase, idea or image relates to the topic of mental health. Write down your thoughts until you have a reaction that is at least 3–5 sentences long.

Feeling Depressed

_____

_____

_____

_____

_____

_____

_____

_____

_____

COLLABORATE AND WRITE ABOUT IT AGAIN

As a team, begin by sharing your individual responses. Then, using a new sheet of paper and your original writings, compose a single mini-essay that represents the team thoughts, feelings and attitudes about the word or phrase. Be prepared to share your work with the class.

REVIEW AND PROCESS

Discuss your team's essay. Talk about your points of agreement and differences of opinion. What kinds of resolutions does your group essay reflect?

Peer View Mirror

Confidence and Me

SURVEY YOUR PEERS

Use the following questions to interview 3 of your friends or peers on the topic of confidence. Use the back of this sheet to record the responses. Use the steps at the bottom of this sheet to tally and discuss your survey results.

SURVEY QUESTIONS

1. Are you a confident person?

2. What helps build your confidence?

3. Name a confident person you admire.

ANALYZE AND CONCLUDE

1. As a class, tally the results of your survey questions on the board.

2. Examine the results and discuss any obvious trends, patterns or unexpected responses.

3. For each question, formulate a conclusion based on the responses. Post the conclusions in a visible spot to refer to during this unit of study.

Being Honest and Mental Health

YOUR CHALLENGE

Use what you know and are learning about self-esteem and mental health to tell your peers how being honest with oneself can help a person stay mentally healthy.

THINK ABOUT IT

- Being honest with yourself can mean facing some very uncomfortable or painful facts. It is sometimes the toughest kind of real you can be!
- Being honest with yourself may require you to ask others for help.
- Being honest with yourself requires some straightforward thinking, without game playing or defense mechanisms.

DESIGN AND DELIVER

Using the Challenge and Think About It statements, design and deliver a P.A. system campaign to educate and motivate your peers to demonstrate the self-honesty that will help their mental health.

PROJECT STEPS

1. Work as a class to brainstorm a list of the kinds of ideas, themes and basic information that would help your peers and friends recognize and value the role that being honest with oneself plays in helping a person stay mentally healthy.

2. Work as collaborative groups to design least 3 appropriate messages that could be part of a week-long P.A. campaign.

3. As a class, select the best messages and some announcers for the campaign.

4. Practice with the P.A. system after school.

5. Deliver and evaluate the effectiveness of the campaign.

Mental Health

The Call Is For You

Dealing with Stress

COLLABORATE AND ADVISE

As a group, take the phone call of a peer in need of help and advice. Work to problem-solve the scenario assigned to your group. Put yourself in the caller's place. Offer the healthiest advice you can. Be ready to share and discuss your responses with the class.

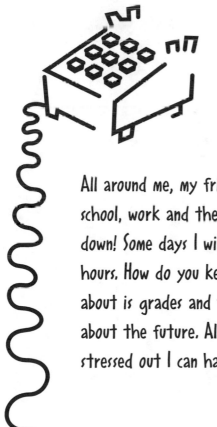

Caller #1

Why Can't I Be Like Them...

All around me, my friends seem to be handling what life is dealing out. But school, work and the expectations people have of me are just wearing me down! Some days I wish it would all just go away, even just for a few hours. How do you keep your balance when all parents and teachers talk about is grades and test scores and "the future"! I'm tired of hearing about the future. All I want to deal with is "right now." Some days I'm so stressed out I can hardly think. What can I do?

Think, Choose, Act Healthy

明 知 Healthy Haiku

Believing in You

THINK, FOCUS AND EXPRESS

Using haiku format, compose a poem about believing in yourself. Present the issues, images or emotions that you think are a part of this challenge. Use the form below to help you write your haiku. Be ready to read and post your work.

Haiku

Five short syl-la-bles,
then fol-low with sev-en more.
Five a-gain, the end.

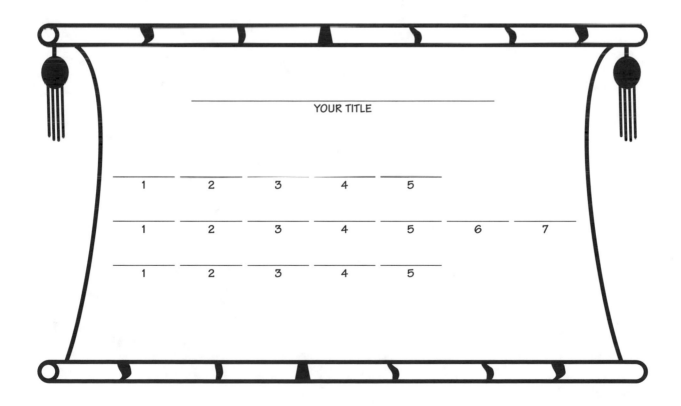

YOUR TITLE

1	2	3	4	5		
1	2	3	4	5	6	7
1	2	3	4	5		

How to Be Good to Yourself

THINK AND PRESCRIBE

Consider all you know about how important it is for people to take care of themselves mentally and emotionally as well as physically. Generate a list of tips or advice to help people treat themselves well.

How to Be Good to Yourself

PFER CLINIC

1. _____
2. _____
3. _____
4. _____
5. _____
6. _____
7. _____
8. _____
9. _____
10. _____

Dr. _____ YOUR NAME

Mental Health

Steps Toward My Future

Liking and Accepting Who I Am

CONSIDER, GENERATE AND APPLY

Think about the healthy goal in the center of the activity sheet. List as many resources and behaviors as you can think of that will help you build your path toward this goal. Use this information to complete the "steps" on the next page. Share and discuss your work. Finalize your responses and post your activity sheet as directed.

Liking and Accepting Who I Am

The attitudes that will help get me here:
_____
_____
_____
_____

The knowledge that will help get me here:
_____
_____
_____
_____

The skills that will help get me here:
_____
_____
_____

The people that will help get me here:
_____
_____
_____

···Continued

Think, Choose, Act Healthy

Continued ....

Mental Health

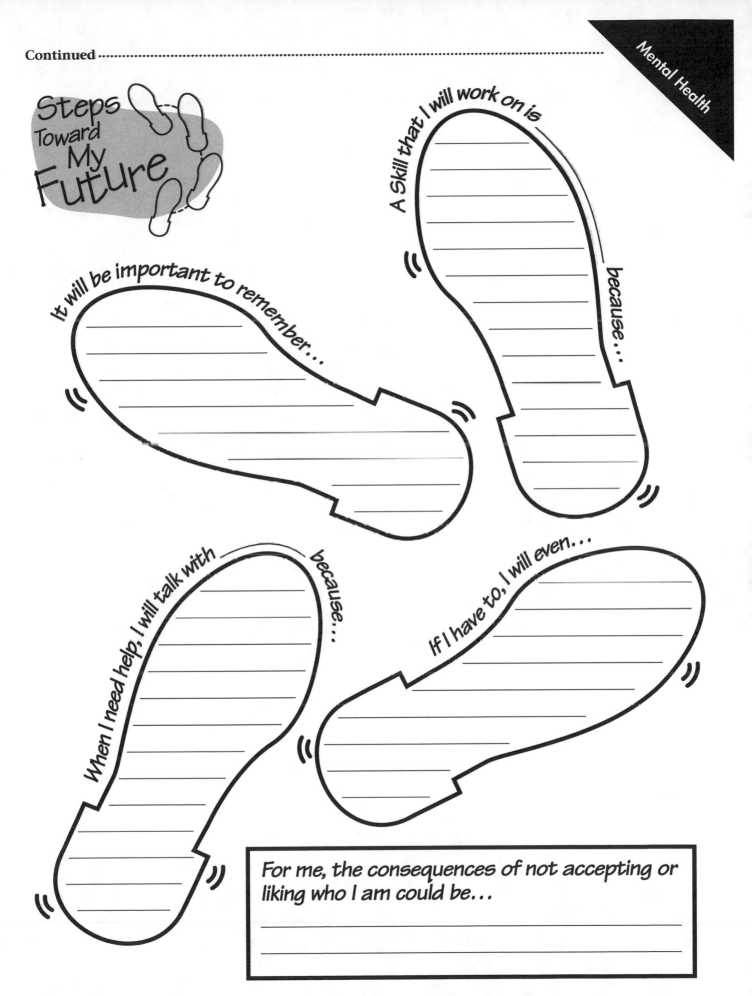

Steps Toward My Future

A Skill that I will work on is

_____
_____
_____
_____
_____

because...

_____
_____
_____

It will be important to remember...

_____
_____
_____
_____
_____

When I need help, I will talk with

_____
_____
_____
_____
_____

because...

_____
_____

If I have to, I will even...

_____
_____
_____
_____
_____

For me, the consequences of not accepting or liking who I am could be...

_____
_____

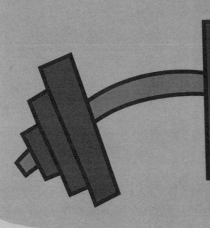

Fitness and Health

Thinking and Talking About Fitness

ASK, LISTEN AND LEARN

Use 1 of the following questions as a **Question Roll Call** prompt (modify if needed). Write the selected question on the board and ask students to think about a response. Call roll. Students use their answer to the question to replace the traditional response of "here" or "present."

1. How high of a priority is fitness in your life?

2. What has your P.E. class taught you about fitness?

3. How will being fit now affect you later in life?

4. Does watching TV affect a person's fitness level? Explain.

5. What is your favorite exercise activity or sport?

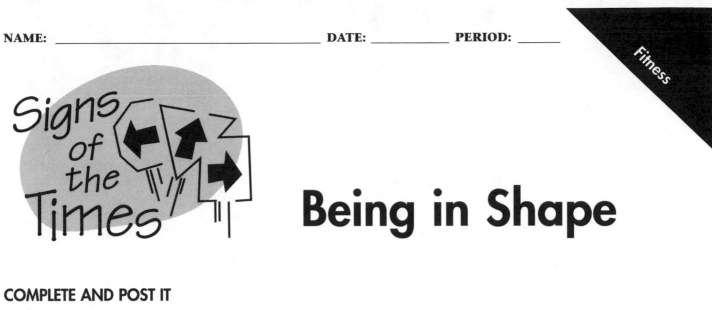

Signs of the Times

Being in Shape

COMPLETE AND POST IT

Carefully read and complete the sign by filling in what you think are some of the attitudes, practices or beliefs that have followed the subject of being in shape through time. Post your work as directed.

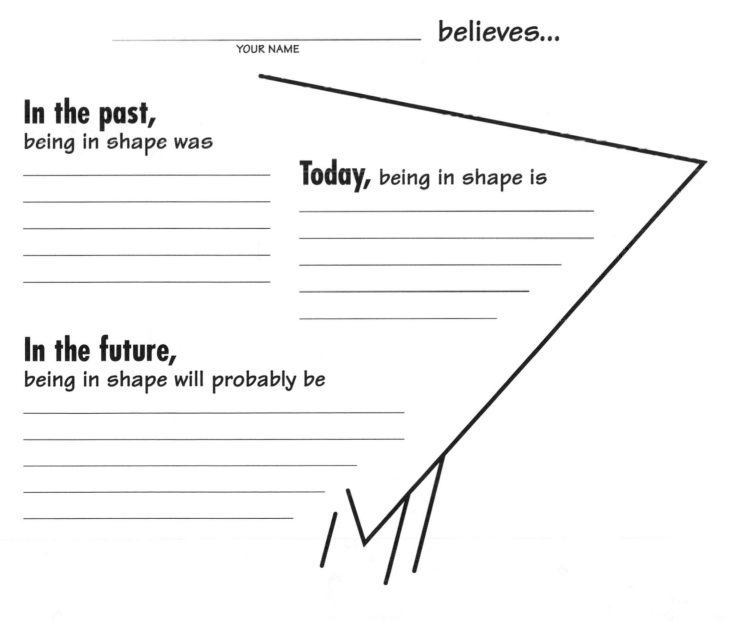

_____ believes...

YOUR NAME

In the past,
being in shape was

_____

_____

_____

_____

Today, being in shape is

_____

_____

_____

_____

In the future,
being in shape will probably be

_____

_____

_____

_____

_____

Thinking About Being Fit for Life

Fitness

COLLABORATE AND CREATE

As a group, discuss your reactions to and the issues that you identify with the idea of being fit for life. Use the letters of the words creatively to record the key points of your discussion. You might want to work out a rough draft first. Be prepared to post your work and share it with the class.

F _____

I _____

T _____

F _____

O _____

R _____

L _____

I _____

F _____

E _____

Me and Fitness

READ AND RESPOND

Read the statements and select a "yes" or "no" response for each. Use the last column to describe evidence of your own personal behavior that supports your answer.

Statements	Yes or No?	My Evidence
1. I begin each day with at least 7–8 restful hours of sleep.		
2. I feel good when I exercise.		
3. I make it a point to exercise a minimum of 3 times per week.		
4. I know a sport that I could enjoy for a lifetime.		
5. I limit the number of hours I spend watching TV.		

REVIEW AND RESPOND

Review your responses and evidence. Use the back of this sheet to write at least 7 sentences about the profile of you they reveal. Say what you think or feel about this profile and what impact it has on your health and well-being today as well as in the future.

Fitness

Determination and Fitness

THINK AND ANNOTATE

Take a few moments to think about feeling determined. Annotate the figure to show what this emotion can make a person think, say and do. A sample has been done for you.

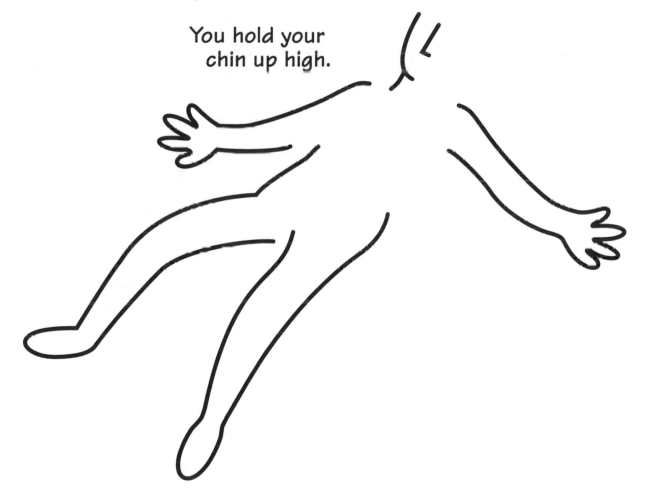

You hold your chin up high.

CONSIDER AND CONCLUDE

State what impact you think determination has on a person's attitude and ability to make healthy changes in personal diet and exercise patterns. Identify some people and personal actions that could help a person maintain this healthy emotion.

Think, Choose, Act Healthy

No Pain, No Gain

THINK AND WRITE

Think about how the following phrase, idea or image relates to the topic of fitness. Write down your thoughts until you have a reaction that is at least 3–5 sentences long.

No Pain, No Gain

_____

_____

_____

_____

_____

_____

_____

_____

_____

COLLABORATE AND WRITE ABOUT IT AGAIN

As a team, begin by sharing your individual responses. Then, using a new sheet of paper and your original writings, compose a single mini-essay that represents the team thoughts, feelings and attitudes about the word or phrase. Be prepared to share your work with the class.

REVIEW AND PROCESS

Discuss your team's essay. Talk about your points of agreement and differences of opinion. What kinds of resolutions does your group essay reflect?

Exercise and Me

SURVEY YOUR PEERS

Use the following questions to interview 3 of your friends or peers on the topic of fitness and exercise. Use the back of this sheet to record the responses. Use the steps at the bottom of this sheet to tally and discuss your survey results.

SURVEY QUESTIONS

1. How high a priority is fitness in your life?

2. What is the greatest payoff of exercise?

3. What kinds of activities do you do to get or stay in shape?

ANALYZE AND CONCLUDE

1. As a class, tally the results of your survey questions on the board.

2. Examine the results and discuss any obvious trends, patterns or unexpected responses.

3. For each question, formulate a conclusion based on the responses. Post the conclusions in a visible spot to refer to during this unit of study.

Fitness

Being Strong and Fit

THINK, FOCUS AND EXPRESS

Using haiku format, compose a poem about being strong and fit. Present the issues, images or emotions that you think are a part of this challenge. Use the form below to help you write your haiku. Be ready to read and post your work.

Haiku

Five short syl-la-bles,
then fol-low with sev-en more.
Five a-gain, the end.

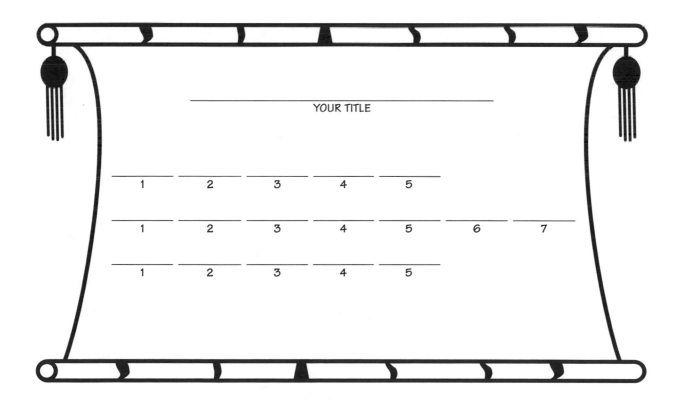

© ETR Associates

How to Put More Exercise in Your Day

THINK AND PRESCRIBE

Consider all you know about the importance of daily exercise. Generate a list of tips and advice to help people find more opportunities to add exercise to their daily schedule.

PEER CLINIC

How to Put More Exercise in Your Day

1. _____
2. _____
3. _____
4. _____
5. _____
6. _____
7. _____
8. _____
9. _____
10. _____

Dr. _____
YOUR NAME

Having a Fit and Healthy Body

CONSIDER, GENERATE AND APPLY

Think about the healthy goal in the center of the activity sheet. List as many resources and behaviors as you can think of that will help you build your path toward this goal. Use this information to complete the "steps" on the next page. Share and discuss your work. Finalize your responses and post your activity sheet as directed.

Having a Fit and Healthy Body

The attitudes that will help get me here:
_____
_____
_____
_____

The knowledge that will help get me here:
_____
_____
_____
_____
_____

The skills that will help get me here:
_____
_____
_____
_____

The people that will help get me here:
_____
_____
_____
_____
_____

···············Continued

Think, Choose, Act Healthy

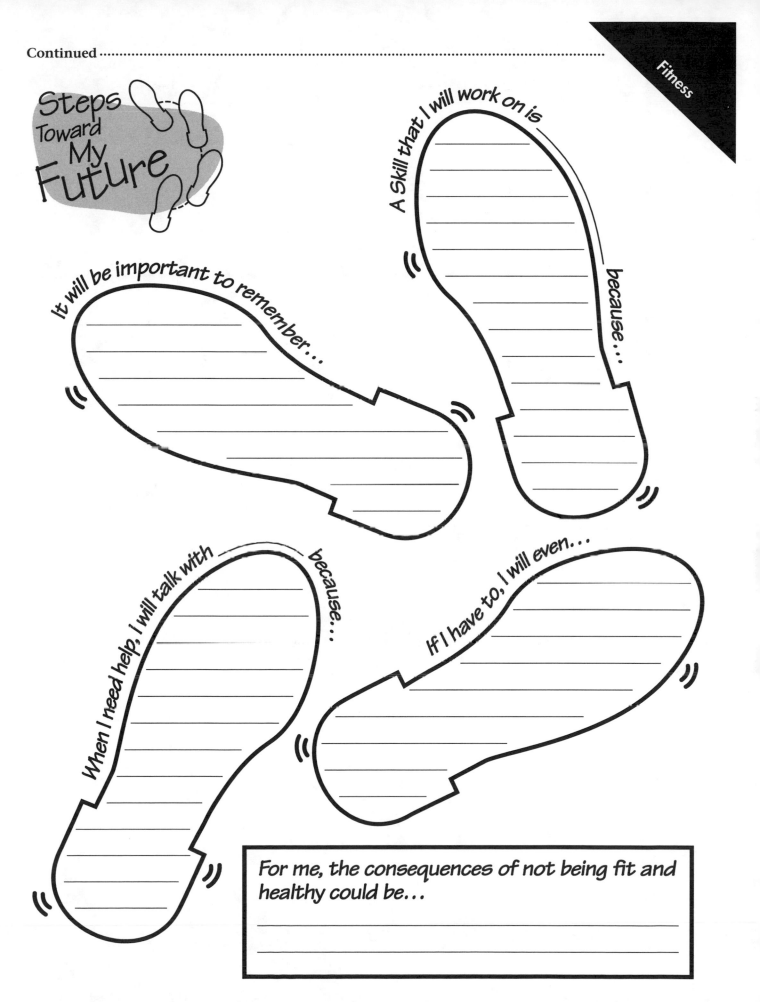

Steps Toward My Future

A Skill that I will work on is

_____
_____
_____
_____
_____
_____

because...

_____
_____

It will be important to remember...

_____
_____
_____
_____
_____
_____

When I need help, I will talk with

_____
_____
_____
_____
_____
_____
_____

because...

If I have to, I will even...

_____
_____
_____
_____
_____
_____

For me, the consequences of not being fit and healthy could be...

_____
_____

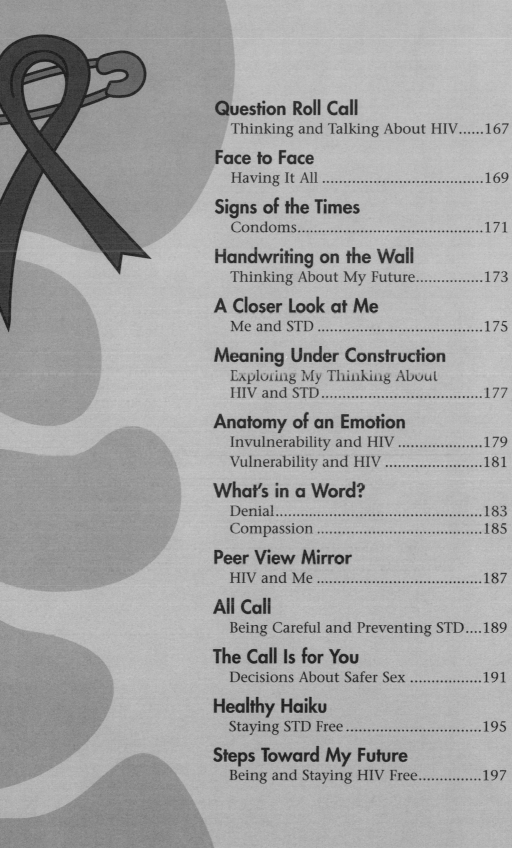

HIV and STD

Thinking and Talking About HIV

ASK, LISTEN AND LEARN

Use 1 of the following questions as a **Question Roll Call** prompt (modify if needed). Write the selected question on the board and ask students to think about a response. Call roll. Students use their answer to the question to replace the traditional response of "here" or "present."

1. Are people today as concerned about HIV as they were a few years ago?

2. What kinds of situations make people forget about the seriousness of HIV?

3. Today, who is doing the best job of educating about HIV?

4. What challenges might you face being friends with an HIV-positive person?

5. Should we be working on a cure for AIDS or an HIV vaccine?

Think, Choose, Act Healthy

HIV and STD

Having It All

READ, THINK AND DISCUSS

I hear what you're saying—
Yeah, I'm young...I'm strong...I got a life ahead of me...
Got talent too. People say I can be anything I want.
Can't you just see me?
Got good friends too...
Be-there-for-you, Stand-by-you, Bring-it-to-me kinds of friends...
Forever friends...
For-ever.
Hey, you know the part that really gets me?
How it's called *"being positive"*!
So, do you think you could tell me just one more time...
The part about being all I can be.
Even now? Now that I'm livin' with HIV.

HIV

CONSTRUCT YOUR OWN MEANING

As a class, discuss the reading by first sharing your initial reactions. Then identify the issues involved in this situation.

Signs of the Times

Condoms

COMPLETE AND POST IT

Carefully read and complete the sign by filling in what you think are the attitudes, practices or beliefs that have followed the subject of condoms through time. Post your work as directed.

_____ **believes...**

YOUR NAME

In the past, *condoms were*

_____
_____
_____
_____
_____

Today, *condoms are*

_____
_____
_____
_____

In the future,
condoms will probably be

_____
_____
_____

HIV and STD

Thinking About My Future

COLLABORATE AND CREATE

As a group, discuss your reactions to and the issues you identify with the idea of your future. Use the letters of the words creatively to record the key points of your discussion. You might want to work out a rough draft first. Be prepared to post your work and share it with the class.

M _____

Y _____

F _____

U _____

T _____

U _____

R _____

E _____

Me and STD

READ AND RESPOND

Read the statements and select a "yes" or "no" response for each. Use the last column to describe evidence of your own personal behavior that supports your answer.

Statements	Yes or No?	My Evidence
1. I understand the consequences of sexually transmitted disease.		
2. I know what the words "casual contact" mean.		
3. I am aware of the only 100% sure way to protect myself from STD.		
4. I know where I can go in my community to get tested for STD.		
5. I know what behaviors put people at risk for HIV infection.		

REVIEW AND RESPOND

Review your responses and evidence. Use the back of this sheet to write at least 7 sentences about the profile of you they reveal. Say what you think or feel about this profile and what impact it has on your health and well-being today as well as in the future.

Think, Choose, Act Healthy

Exploring My Thinking About HIV and STD

HIV and STD

THINK, SELECT AND RESPOND

Use this sheet during your lesson(s) about HIV and STD. At the teacher's signal, select and complete the prompt that best fits your personal thinking at the time. Be prepared to share your thoughts with others.

I think the HIV epidemic is...

Teens and STD...

I was surprised to find out that...

In my opinion, HIV and STD are...

The best way to fight HIV/STD infection is...

I still want to understand...

When I hear someone is HIV positive, I think or feel...

Invulnerability and HIV

THINK AND ANNOTATE

Take a few moments to think about feeling invulnerable. Annotate the figure to show what this emotion can make a person think, say and do. A sample has been done for you.

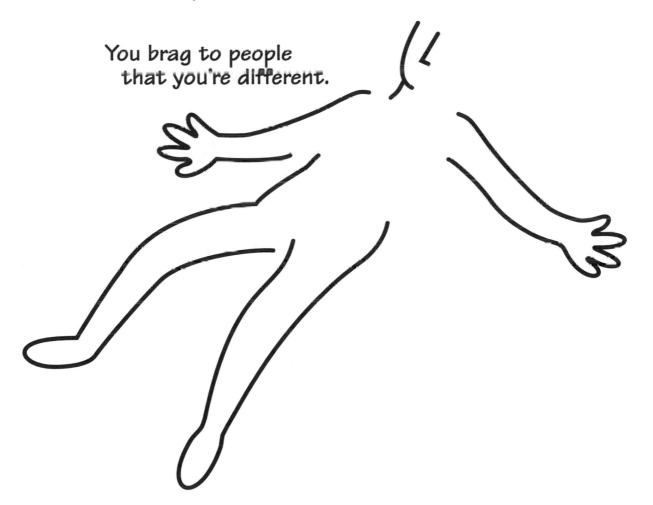

You brag to people that you're different.

CONSIDER AND CONCLUDE

State what impact you think feeling invulnerable has on people's attitudes and ability to make healthy choices about behaviors that put them at risk for HIV. Identify some people and personal actions that could help a person cope with this emotion in a healthy way.

Think, Choose, Act Healthy

Vulnerability and HIV

THINK AND ANNOTATE

Take a few moments to think about feeling vulnerable. Annotate the figure to show what this emotion can make a person think, say and do. A sample has been done for you.

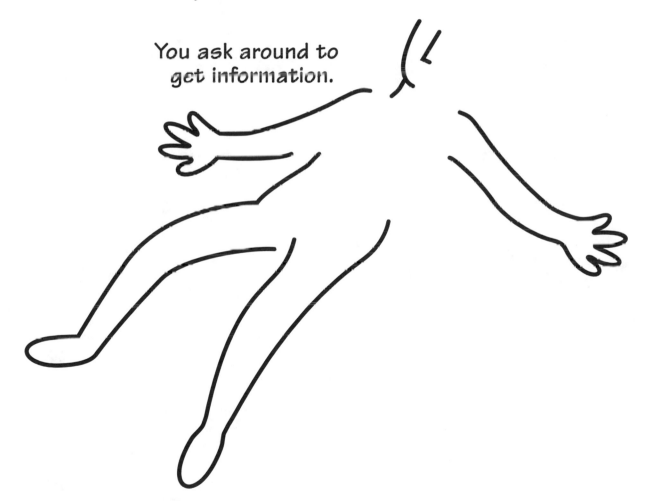

You ask around to get information.

CONSIDER AND CONCLUDE

State what impact you think feeling vulnerable has on people's attitudes and ability to make healthy choices about behaviors that put them at risk for HIV. Identify some people and personal actions that could help a person maintain this emotion in a healthy way.

Think, Choose, Act Healthy

Denial

THINK AND WRITE

Think about how the following word, idea or image relates to the topic of HIV and STD. Write down your thoughts until you have a reaction that is at least 3–5 sentences long.

_____

_____

_____

_____

_____

_____

_____

_____

_____

COLLABORATE AND WRITE ABOUT IT AGAIN

As a team, begin by sharing your individual responses. Then, using a new sheet of paper and your original writings, compose a single mini-essay that represents the team thoughts, feelings and attitudes about the word or phrase. Be prepared to share your work with the class.

REVIEW AND PROCESS

Discuss your team's essay. Talk about your points of agreement and differences of opinion. What kinds of resolutions does your group essay reflect?

Compassion

THINK AND WRITE

Think about how the following word, idea or image relates to the topic of HIV and STD. Write down your thoughts until you have a reaction that is at least 3–5 sentences long.

_____

_____

_____

_____

_____

_____

_____

_____

_____

COLLABORATE AND WRITE ABOUT IT AGAIN

As a team, begin by sharing your individual responses. Then, using a new sheet of paper and your original writings, compose a single mini-essay that represents the team thoughts, feelings and attitudes about the word or phrase. Be prepared to share your work with the class.

REVIEW AND PROCESS

Discuss your team's essay. Talk about your points of agreement and differences of opinion. What kinds of resolutions does your group essay reflect?

HIV and Me

SURVEY YOUR PEERS

Use the following questions to interview 3 of your friends or peers on the topic of HIV. Use the back of this sheet to record the responses. Use the steps at the bottom of this sheet to tally and discuss your survey results.

SURVEY QUESTIONS

1. Do you think that you are well informed about HIV?

2. How much do you and your friends talk about the risk of HIV?

3. Where has most of your information about HIV come from?

ANALYZE AND CONCLUDE

1. As a class, tally the results of your survey questions on the board.

2. Examine the results and discuss any obvious trends, patterns or unexpected responses.

3. For each question, formulate a conclusion based on the responses. Post the conclusions in a visible spot to refer to during this unit of study.

Being Careful and Preventing STD

YOUR CHALLENGE

Use what you know and are learning about STD to tell your peers how being careful can help people prevent STD infection.

THINK ABOUT IT

- Being careful is not just about concern for yourself. It means you also consider the well-being of others.
- Being careful requires you to use all of your knowledge, skills and healthy attitudes to bring about positive outcomes.
- Being careful about HIV infection has the power to save lives.

DESIGN AND DELIVER

Using the Challenge and Think About It statements, design and deliver a P.A. system campaign to educate and motivate your peers to demonstrate the careful thoughts and actions that can help prevent STD.

PROJECT STEPS

1. Work as a class to brainstorm a list of the kinds of ideas, themes and basic information that would help your peers and friends recognize and value the role being careful plays in preventing STD.

2. Work as collaborative groups to design at least 3 appropriate messages that could be part of a week-long P.A. campaign.

3. As a class, select the best messages and some announcers for the campaign.

4. Practice with the P.A. system after school.

5. Deliver and evaluate the effectiveness of the campaign.

Decisions About Safer Sex

COLLABORATE AND ADVISE

As a group, take the phone call of a peer in need of help and advice. Work to problem-solve the scenario assigned to your group. Put yourself in the caller's place. Offer the healthiest advice you can. Be ready to share and discuss your responses with the class.

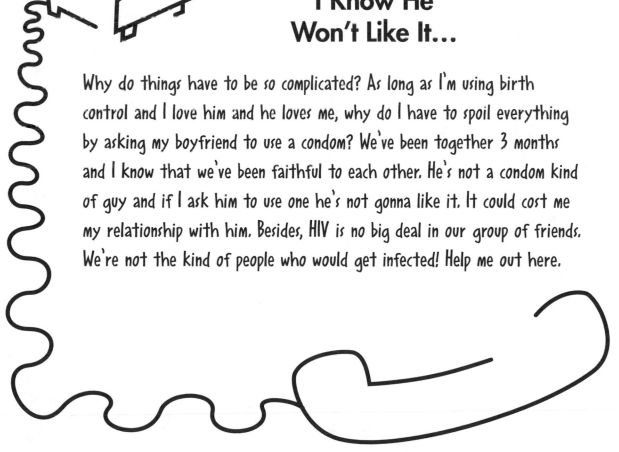

Caller #1

I Know He Won't Like It...

Why do things have to be so complicated? As long as I'm using birth control and I love him and he loves me, why do I have to spoil everything by asking my boyfriend to use a condom? We've been together 3 months and I know that we've been faithful to each other. He's not a condom kind of guy and if I ask him to use one he's not gonna like it. It could cost me my relationship with him. Besides, HIV is no big deal in our group of friends. We're not the kind of people who would get infected! Help me out here.

•••Continued

Decisions About Safer Sex

Caller #2

Help Me Find the Way to Ask...

It feels great to be around her. Sometimes I think my heart's gonna explode. We've moved beyond hand holding and kissing as a way to show we care and I think we're ready to have sex. I'm sure it's what we both want. The thing is, I can't seem to find the words to ask the questions I'm supposed to ask about what we've done in the past with other people. I'm sure we're both OK. And I don't want to insult her or hurt her feelings. Maybe we don't even need to have this talk. What do you think?

Staying STD Free

THINK, FOCUS AND EXPRESS

Using haiku format, compose a poem about staying STD free. Present the issues, images or emotions that you think are a part of this challenge. Use the form below to help you write your haiku. Be ready to read and post your work.

Haiku

Five short syl-la-bles,
then fol-low with sev-en more.
Five a-gain, the end.

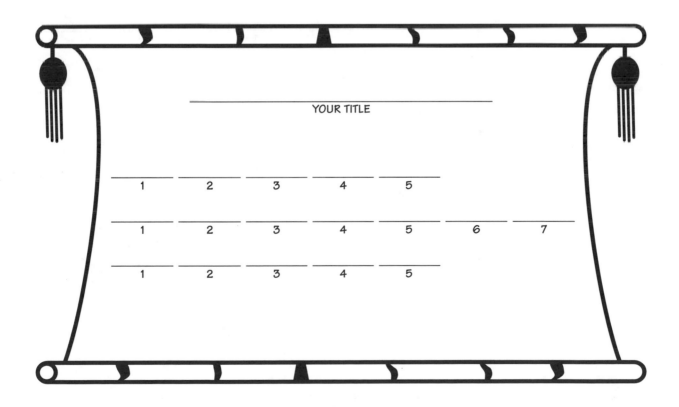

YOUR TITLE

1   2   3   4   5

1   2   3   4   5   6   7

1   2   3   4   5

Being and Staying HIV Free

CONSIDER, GENERATE AND APPLY

Think about the healthy goal in the center of the activity sheet. List as many resources and behaviors as you can think of that will help you build your path toward this goal. Use this information to complete the "steps" on the next page. Share and discuss your work. Finalize your responses and post your activity sheet as directed.

Being and Staying HIV Free

The attitudes that will help get me here:
_____
_____
_____
_____

The knowledge that will help get me here:
_____
_____
_____
_____

The people that will help get me here:
_____
_____
_____
_____

The skills that will help get me here:
_____
_____
_____
_____

Continued

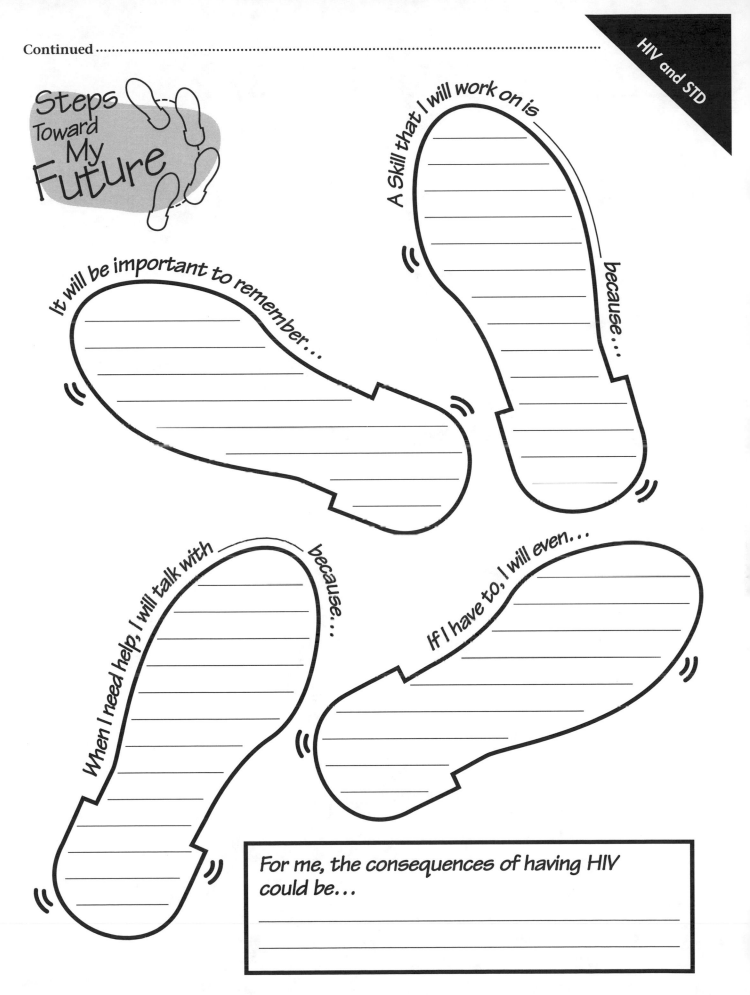

Steps
Toward
My
Future

A Skill that I will work on is

_____
_____
_____
_____
_____
_____
_____

because…
_____
_____
_____

It will be important to remember…

_____
_____
_____
_____
_____

When I need help, I will talk with

_____

because…
_____
_____
_____
_____
_____

If I have to, I will even…

_____
_____
_____
_____
_____

For me, the consequences of having HIV could be…

_____
_____

Sexuality and Relationships

Thinking and Talking About Relationships

ASK, LISTEN AND LEARN

Use 1 of the following questions as a **Question Roll Call** prompt (modify if needed). Write the selected question on the board and ask students to think about a response. Call roll. Students use their answer to the question to replace the traditional response of "here" or "present."

Friendship

1. Why do people become friends?

2. How many good friends can a person have?

3. What happens when friends become more important than family?

4. What are some reasons that friendships end?

5. What is a sure way to keep a friendship healthy and alive?

Dating

6. Why do people date?

7. What are some good dating rules?

8. What happens when people misunderstand the meaning of or reason for a date?

9. What are some good date activities?

10. How important is it for both people to meet each other's parents?

Families

11. What is one thing your family always does the same?

12. Name the people in your family.

13. What is the most important thing your family wants for you?

14. Will you choose to raise a family some day? how large?

15. When things are tough, whom in your family do you talk with?

Think, Choose, Act Healthy

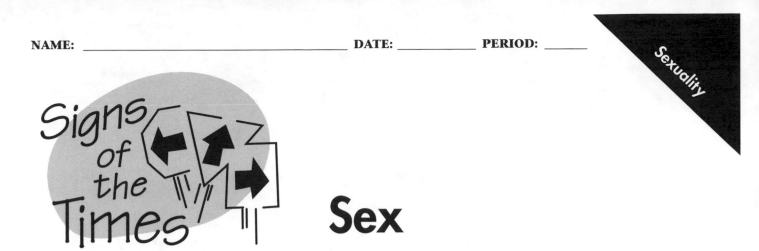

Sexuality

Sex

COMPLETE AND POST IT

Carefully read and complete the sign by filling in what you think are some of the attitudes, practices or beliefs that have followed the subject of sex through time. Post your work as directed.

_____ **believes...**
YOUR NAME

In the past, sex was

_____

_____

_____

_____

_____

Today, sex is

_____

_____

_____

_____

_____

In the future,
sex will probably be

_____

_____

_____

Teen Pregnancy

Teen Pregnancy

COMPLETE AND POST IT

Carefully read and complete the sign by filling in what you think are some of the attitudes, practices or beliefs that have followed the subject of teen pregnancy through time. Post your work as directed.

_____ **believes...**
YOUR NAME

In the past,
teen pregnancy was

_____

_____

_____

_____

Today, teen pregnancy is

_____

_____

_____

_____

In the future,
teen pregnancy will probably be

_____

_____

_____

Think, Choose, Act Healthy

Relationships

Signs of the Times

Families

COMPLETE AND POST IT

Carefully read and complete the sign by filling in what you think are some of the attitudes, practices or beliefs that have followed the subject of families through time. Post your work as directed.

_____ **believes...**
YOUR NAME

In the past,
families were

_____
_____
_____
_____

Today, families are

_____
_____
_____
_____

In the future,
families will probably be

_____
_____
_____
_____
_____

Relationships

Thinking About Friends

COLLABORATE AND CREATE

As a group, discuss your reactions to and the issues you identify with friends. Use the letters of the words creatively to record the key points of your discussion. You might want to work out a rough draft first. Be prepared to post your work and share it with the class.

F _____

R _____

I _____

E _____

N _____

D _____

S _____

Me and Sexuality

READ AND RESPOND

Read the statements and select a "yes" or "no" response for each. Use the last column to provide evidence of your own personal behavior that supports your answer.

Statements	Yes or No?	My Evidence
1. I feel comfortable talking and asking questions about human sexuality.		
2. I can cope with the mood swings that are part of changing and growing.		
3. I am aware of and practice the self-exams that are a part of sexual health.		
4. I know the responsibilities that come with sexual maturity.		
5. I do not stereotype people based on their gender.		

REVIEW AND RESPOND

Review your responses and evidence. Use the back of this sheet to write at least 7 sentences about the profile of you they reveal. Say what you think or feel about this profile and what impact it has on your health and well-being today as well as in the future.

Me and Teen Pregnancy

READ AND RESPOND

Read the statements and select a "yes" or "no" response for each. Use the last column to describe evidence of your own personal behavior that supports your answer.

Statements	Yes or No?	My Evidence
1. I'm aware of how teen pregnancy would affect my present life.		
2. I'm aware of how teen pregnancy would affect my future.		
3. I know the other risks of sexual activity besides pregnancy.		
4. I have a sense of what it means to be a parent.		
5. I know the only 100% sure way to protect myself from pregnancy.		

REVIEW AND RESPOND

Review your responses and evidence. Use the back of this sheet to write at least 7 sentences about the profile of you they reveal. Say what you think or feel about this profile and what impact it has on your health and well-being today as well as in the future.

Think, Choose, Act Healthy

Exploring My Thinking About Sexuality

Meaning Under Construction

Sexuality

THINK, SELECT AND RESPOND

Use this sheet during your lesson(s) about sexuality. At the teacher's signal, select and complete the prompt that best fits your personal thinking at the time. Be prepared to share your thoughts with others.

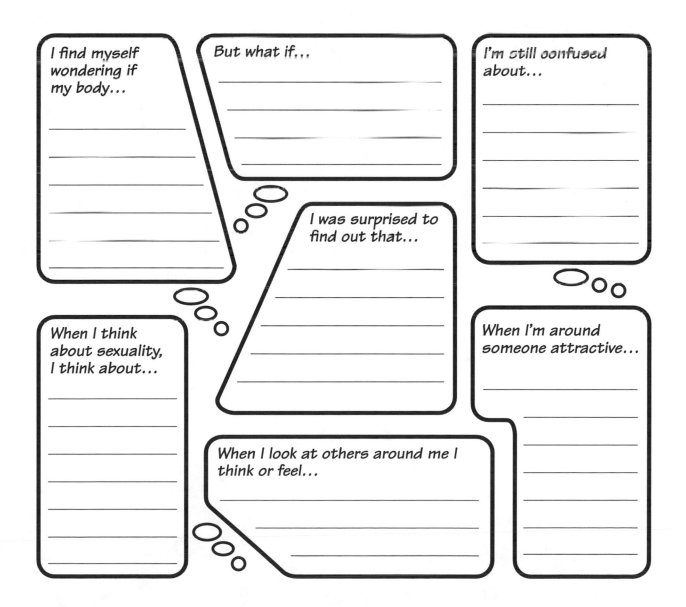

I find myself wondering if my body...

But what if...

I'm still confused about...

I was surprised to find out that...

When I think about sexuality, I think about...

When I'm around someone attractive...

When I look at others around me I think or feel...

Exploring My Thinking About Relationships

Relationships

THINK, SELECT AND RESPOND

Use this sheet during your lesson(s) about relationships. At the teacher's signal, select and complete the prompt that best fits your personal thinking at the time. Be prepared to share your thoughts with others.

People like me because...
_____
_____
_____
_____
_____

I try to be like _____ because...
_____
_____
_____
_____

My greatest friend has been...
_____
_____
_____
_____
_____

Most teachers think I...
_____
_____
_____
_____

A relationship I'm sorry I lost was...
_____
_____
_____
_____
_____

My parents would say that I...
_____
_____
_____
_____

In my opinion, when good friends argue...
_____
_____
_____

Think, Choose, Act Healthy

Anatomy of an Emotion

Confidence and Sexuality

THINK AND ANNOTATE

Take a few moments to think about feeling confident. Annotate the figure to show what this emotion can make a person think, say and do. A sample has been done for you.

You hold your shoulders back and stand up straight.

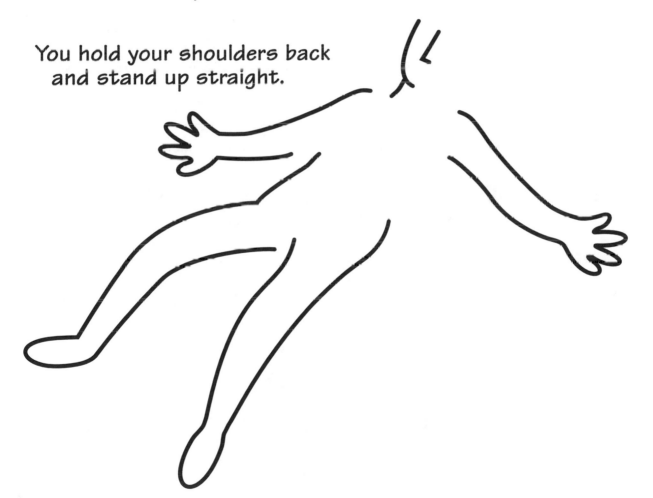

CONSIDER AND CONCLUDE

State what impact you think confidence has on a person's attitude and ability to accept the physical and sexual changes of growing up as positive experiences. Identify some people and personal actions that could help a person maintain this healthy emotion.

Having a Crush

THINK AND WRITE

Think about how the following phrase, idea or image relates to the topic of relationships. Write down your thoughts until you have a reaction that is at least 3–5 sentences long.

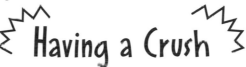

_____

_____

_____

_____

_____

_____

_____

_____

COLLABORATE AND WRITE ABOUT IT AGAIN

As a team, begin by sharing your individual responses. Then, using a new sheet of paper and your original writings, compose a single mini-essay that represents the team thoughts, feelings and attitudes about the word or phrase. Be prepared to share your work with the class.

REVIEW AND PROCESS

Discuss your team's essay. Talk about your points of agreement and differences of opinion. What kinds of resolutions does your group essay reflect?

Relationships

Family

THINK AND WRITE

Think about how the following word, idea or image relates to the topic of relationships. Write down your thoughts until you have a reaction that is at least 3–5 sentences long.

Family

_____

_____

_____

_____

_____

_____

_____

_____

COLLABORATE AND WRITE ABOUT IT AGAIN

As a team, begin by sharing your individual responses. Then, using a new sheet of paper and your original writings, compose a single mini-essay that represents the team thoughts, feelings and attitudes about the word or phrase. Be prepared to share your work with the class.

REVIEW AND PROCESS

Discuss your team's essay. Talk about your points of agreement and differences of opinion. What kinds of resolutions does your group essay reflect?

The Teen Years and Me

SURVEY YOUR PEERS

Use the following questions to interview 3 of your friends or peers on the topic of being a teenager. Use the back of this sheet to record the responses. Use the steps at the bottom of this sheet to tally and discuss your survey results.

SURVEY QUESTIONS

1. What is the best thing about growing up and changing?

2. What is the toughest thing about growing up and changing?

3. What advice would you give to younger people about these changes?

ANALYZE AND CONCLUDE

1. As a class, tally the results of your survey questions on the board.

2. Examine the results and discuss any obvious trends, patterns or unexpected responses.

3. For each question, formulate a conclusion based on the responses. Post the conclusions in a visible spot to refer to during this unit of study.

Trust, Respect and Me

SURVEY YOUR PEERS

Use the following questions to interview 3 of your friends or peers on the topic of trust and respect. Use the back of this sheet to record the responses. Use the steps at the bottom of this sheet to tally and discuss your survey results.

SURVEY QUESTIONS

1. How do you demonstrate respect for someone?

2. How does a person earn the trust of others?

3. What roles do trust and respect play in relationships?

ANALYZE AND CONCLUDE

1. As a class, tally the results of your survey questions on the board.

2. Examine the results and discuss any obvious trends, patterns or unexpected responses.

3. For each question, formulate a conclusion based on the responses. Post the conclusions in a visible spot to refer to during this unit of study.

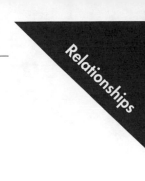

Friends and Me

SURVEY YOUR PEERS

Use the following questions to interview 3 of your friends or peers on the topic of friendship. Use the back of this sheet to record the responses. Use the steps at the bottom of this sheet to tally and discuss your survey results.

SURVEY QUESTIONS

1. How important is it to have friends?

2. What will a real friend do for you?

3. In what ways can friends also be your worst enemies?

ANALYZE AND CONCLUDE

1. As a class, tally the results of your survey questions on the board.

2. Examine the results and discuss any obvious trends, patterns or unexpected responses.

3. For each question, formulate a conclusion based on the responses. Post the conclusions in a visible spot to refer to during this unit of study.

Sexuality

Being Self-Reliant and Having a Healthy Sexual Self-Image

YOUR CHALLENGE

Use what you know and are learning about sexuality to tell your peers how being self-reliant can help people maintain a healthy sexual self-image that is not dictated by the media.

THINK ABOUT IT

- The media (movies, TV, music, videos, magazines) tend to portray sexuality as the most important aspect of being a person.
- Self-reliant people have confidence and trust in their own view of who they are and what defines them.
- Being self-reliant can positively influence a person's expression of and attitude toward sexuality, both of self and others.

DESIGN AND DELIVER

Using the Challenge and Think About It statements, design and deliver a P.A. system campaign to educate and motivate your peers to maintain healthy sexual self-image that is not dictated by the media.

PROJECT STEPS

1. Work as a class to brainstorm a list of the kinds of ideas, themes and basic information that would help your peers and friends recognize and value the role being self-reliant plays in maintaining a healthy sexual self-image that is not dictated by the media.

2. Work as collaborative groups to design at least 3 appropriate messages that could be part of a week-long P.A. campaign.

3. As a class, select the best messages and some announcers for the campaign.

4. Practice with the P.A. system after school.

5. Deliver and evaluate the effectiveness of the campaign.

Think, Choose, Act Healthy

Teen Pregnancy

Being Responsible and Avoiding Teen Pregnancy

YOUR CHALLENGE

Use what you know and are learning about sexuality and relationships to tell your peers how being responsible can help protect teens from unwanted pregnancy.

THINK ABOUT IT

- Being responsible means being accountable for your choices and behaviors, and their impact on you and those around you.
- Being responsible is about being able to distinguish between right and wrong.
- Being responsible is a key behavior associated with being mature.

DESIGN AND DELIVERY

Using the Challenge and Think About Statements, design and deliver a P.A. system campaign to educate and motivate peers to demonstrate the personal responsibility that helps teens avoid unwanted pregnancy.

PROJECT STEPS

1. Work as a class to brainstorm a list of the kinds of ideas, themes and basic information that would help your friends and peers recognize and value the role responsible thinking and behavior play in avoiding unwanted pregnancy.

2. Work as collaborative groups to design at least 3 appropriate messages that could be part of a week-long P.A. campaign.

3. As a class, select the best messages and some announcers for the campaign.

4. Practice with the P.A. system after school.

5. Deliver and evaluate the effectiveness of the campaign.

The Call Is For You

What's Your Image?

COLLABORATE AND ADVISE

As a group, take the phone call of a peer in need of help and advice. Work to problem-solve the scenario assigned to your group. Put yourself in the caller's place. Offer the healthiest advice you can. Be ready to share and discuss your responses with the class.

Caller #1

It's My Own Business How I Dress

I like to wear tight clothes and short skirts! It just means I'm proud of my body and I don't mind showing it off. My friends really have their nerve criticizing me. They say I'm "just asking for it." Asking for what? They're just jealous because guys pay so much attention to me. I'm the one they like to stand next to, talk to, look at...and boy do they look at me! I know they respect me and would never get the wrong idea. Maybe I need to get new friends...

Continued

What's Your Image?

Caller #2

I'm Different...

Sometimes I feel like just staying away from my so-called friends. The guys I hang around with sure make it clear that I don't think like they do. This year all they ever talk about is sex. They act like nothing else matters. They tell stories like they are doing it every single day. Some of the girls I know would die if they knew what was said behind their backs. The guys have started to notice that I don't join in and they don't like that. Sometimes they start in on me, like there's something wrong with me. Is there? Is this just the way it's supposed to be with guys?

Tough Decisions

COLLABORATE AND ADVISE

As a group, take the phone call of a peer in need of help and advice. Work to problem-solve the scenario assigned to your group. Put yourself in the caller's place. Offer the healthiest advice you can. Be ready to share and discuss your responses with the class.

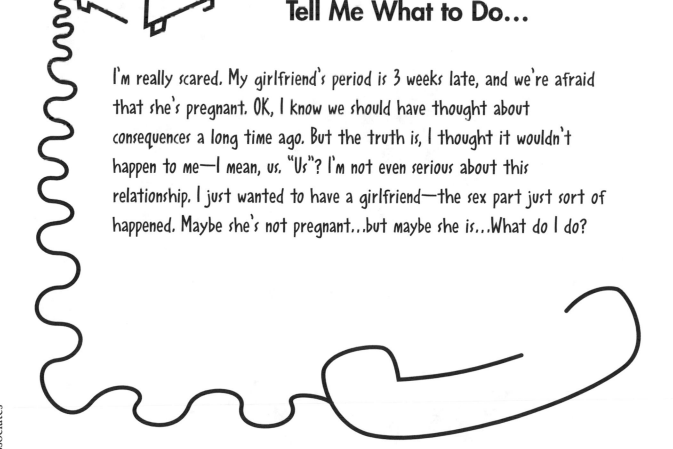

Caller #1

Tell Me What to Do...

I'm really scared. My girlfriend's period is 3 weeks late, and we're afraid that she's pregnant. OK, I know we should have thought about consequences a long time ago. But the truth is, I thought it wouldn't happen to me—I mean, us. "Us"? I'm not even serious about this relationship. I just wanted to have a girlfriend—the sex part just sort of happened. Maybe she's not pregnant...but maybe she is...What do I do?

Tough Decisions

Caller #2

She Says It Would Make Her Proud...

Lots of guys in my group of friends have fathered babies. They make it seem like it's no big deal. My girlfriend has been pressuring me to get her pregnant. She says it would make her proud to have a baby that was mine. She says it would prove to everybody how serious we are about each other. I really care about her, and I guess babies are kind of cute. What would you do?

Getting Along

Relationships

COLLABORATE AND ADVISE

As a group, take the phone call of a peer in need of help and advice. Work to problem-solve the scenario assigned to your group. Put yourself in the caller's place. Offer the healthiest advice you can. Be ready to share and discuss your responses with the class.

Caller #1

Can He Change?

I kept saying that it didn't really matter...then my friends met my boyfriend. He is really a sweet guy, but he's got a mouth like a trash can. He can't say 3 words without one of them being foul. My friends got real quiet the first time they heard him talk. I could feel them looking at me, like it says something about me too. He says swearing is just a habit. I say habits can be broken. He says that how he chooses to talk is his business and if I try to change him, it's over. Do I give up? Is what I'm asking him to think about and do such a big deal? How should I handle this?

··Continued

Continued ⋯⋯⋯⋯⋯⋯⋯⋯⋯⋯⋯⋯⋯⋯⋯⋯⋯⋯⋯⋯⋯⋯⋯

Getting Along

Caller #2

I Don't Recognize You Anymore...

My mom and I hardly look at each other anymore, let alone talk. With my dad gone, we've been trying to figure out how to be this new 2-person family...but it isn't enough for me. I really depend on my friends these days—people I want to be with and be like. Mom doesn't like it. She says they're changing me, that she doesn't even recognize me anymore, and that I'm destroying what's left of our family. I love my mom but I need my friends too. How can I make this work?

Continued

Getting Along

Caller #3

Let Me Take
Care of Me...

My dad and I have always been close. He's been there for every great and bad moment of my life that I can remember. Some kids would love to be able to say that about their dads. Problem is, I think it's time for Dad to let go of me. I need to go through some stuff alone...just to see how I do. But I'm afraid it's going to break his heart or, worse, he'll think that I don't appreciate everything he's done for me. But he's got such a hold on me and my life...I need to take care of myself now. How do I tell him this without hurting him?

Think, Choose, Act Healthy

Growing Up

THINK, FOCUS AND EXPRESS

Using haiku format, compose a poem about growing up. Present the issues, images or emotions that you think are a part of this challenge. Use the form below to help you write your haiku. Be ready to read and post your work.

Haiku

Five short syl-la-bles,
Then fol-low with sev-en more.
Five a-gain, the end.

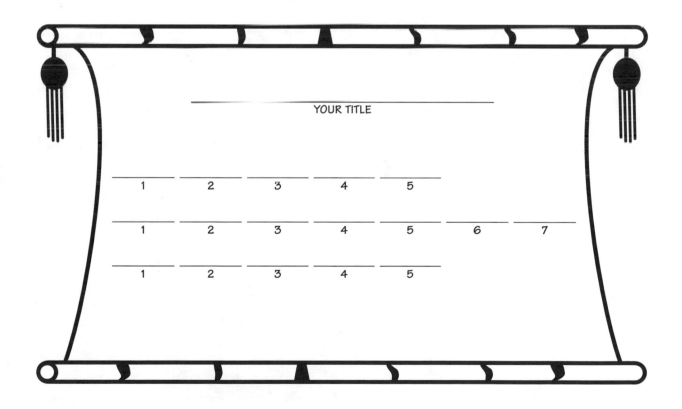

Being a Family

THINK, FOCUS AND EXPRESS

Using haiku format, compose a poem about being a family. Present the issues, images or emotions that you think are a part of this challenge. Use the form below to help you write your haiku. Be ready to read and post your work.

Haiku

Five short syl-la-bles,
then fol-low with sev-en more.
Five a-gain, the end.

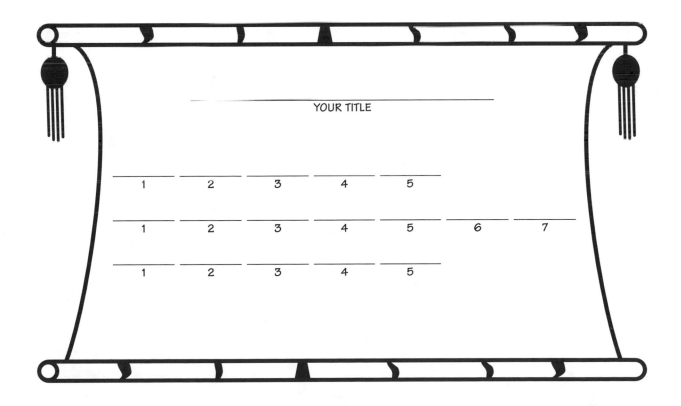

YOUR TITLE

1	2	3	4	5		
1	2	3	4	5	6	7
1	2	3	4	5		

How to Stop Gender Stereotyping

THINK AND PRESCRIBE

Consider what you know about the problems and challenges related to gender stereotyping. Generate a list of tips or advice about attitudes and actions that would help counter this kind of thinking.

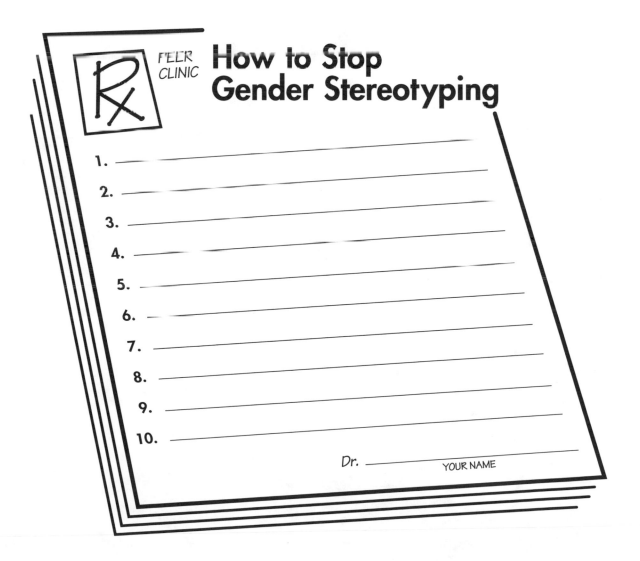

PEER CLINIC How to Stop Gender Stereotyping

1. _____
2. _____
3. _____
4. _____
5. _____
6. _____
7. _____
8. _____
9. _____
10. _____

Dr. _____ YOUR NAME

How to Get Along with Parents and Other Adults

THINK AND PRESCRIBE

Consider what you know about the importance of getting along with parents and other adults. Generate a list of tips or advice for building and maintaining positive relationships with these people.

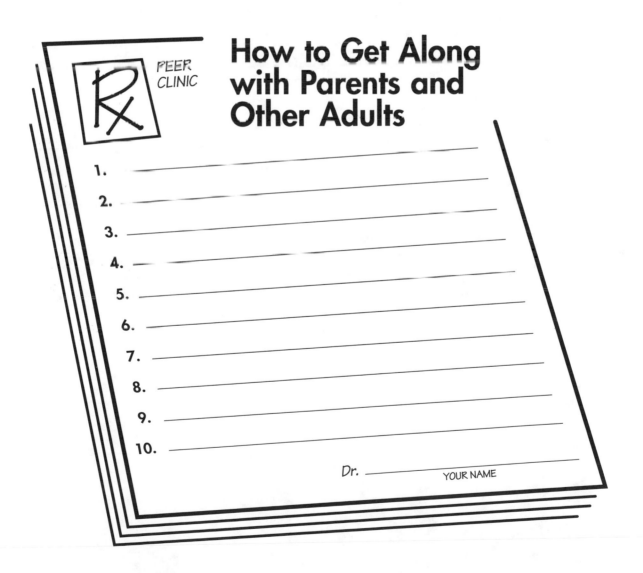

PEER CLINIC

How to Get Along with Parents and Other Adults

1. _____
2. _____
3. _____
4. _____
5. _____
6. _____
7. _____
8. _____
9. _____
10. _____

Dr. _____ YOUR NAME

How to Get to Know Someone You Find Attractive

THINK AND PRESCRIBE

Consider what you know about the pressures or feelings around trying to initiate a relationship with someone you're attracted to. Generate a list of tips or advice to make this a more comfortable and positive experience.

PEER CLINIC

How to Get to Know Someone You Find Attractive

1. _____
2. _____
3. _____
4. _____
5. _____
6. _____
7. _____
8. _____
9. _____
10. _____

Dr. _____
YOUR NAME

Tobacco, Alcohol and Drugs

Thinking and Talking About Drugs

ASK, LISTEN AND LEARN

Use 1 of the following questions as a **Question Roll Call** prompt (modify if needed). Write the selected question on the board and ask students to think about a response. Call roll. Students use their answer to the question to replace the traditional response of "here" or "present."

Tobacco

1. What is 1 consequence of smoking?

2. Why would a so-called friend offer another friend tobacco?

3. What is it like to experience secondhand smoke?

4. Why do many people deny that tobacco is a drug?

5. Can an adult who smokes convince a young person not to?

Alcohol

6. What is 1 way alcohol can affect a teen's life?

7. Why do many people think that alcohol is less risky than drugs?

8. Name an activity (not using alcohol) that would make you feel good.

9. What are some things teens think drinking proves?

10. What is the attitude toward drinking in your school?

Drugs

11. What role does stress play in teen drug use?

12. What is 1 reason to be drug free?

13. What behaviors make you suspect another person of using drugs?

14. How much power does a friend have to save someone from drug use?

15. What effects do "Just say no" campaigns have?

Tobacco

Signs of the Times

Using Tobacco

COMPLETE AND POST IT

Carefully read and complete the sign by filling in what you think are some of the attitudes, practices or beliefs that have followed the subject of tobacco use through time. Post your work as directed.

_____ believes...
YOUR NAME

In the past,
using tobacco was
_____
_____
_____
_____

Today, using tobacco is
_____
_____
_____
_____

In the future,
using tobacco will probably be
_____
_____
_____

Peer Pressure

COMPLETE AND POST IT

Carefully read and complete the sign by filling in what you think are some of the attitudes, practices or beliefs that have followed the subject of peer pressure through time. Post your work as directed.

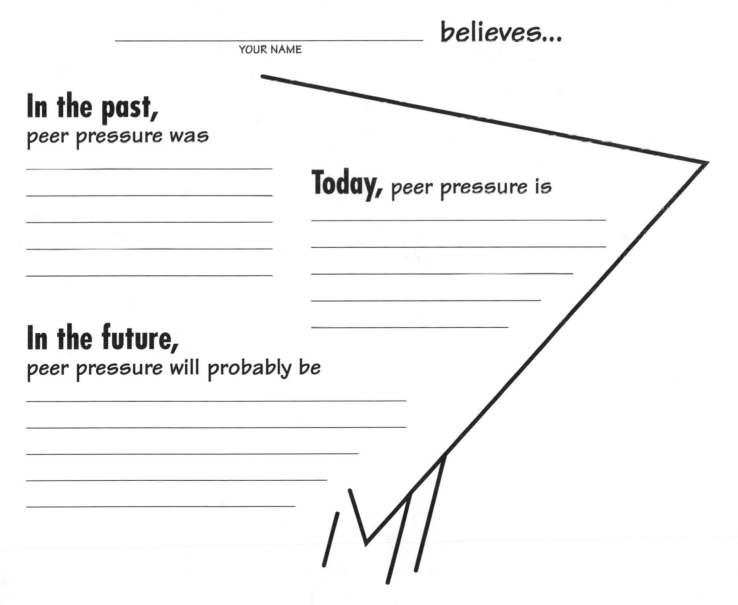

_____ **believes...**
YOUR NAME

In the past,
peer pressure was

_____
_____
_____
_____

Today, peer pressure is

_____
_____
_____
_____

In the future,
peer pressure will probably be

_____
_____
_____
_____

Signs of the Times

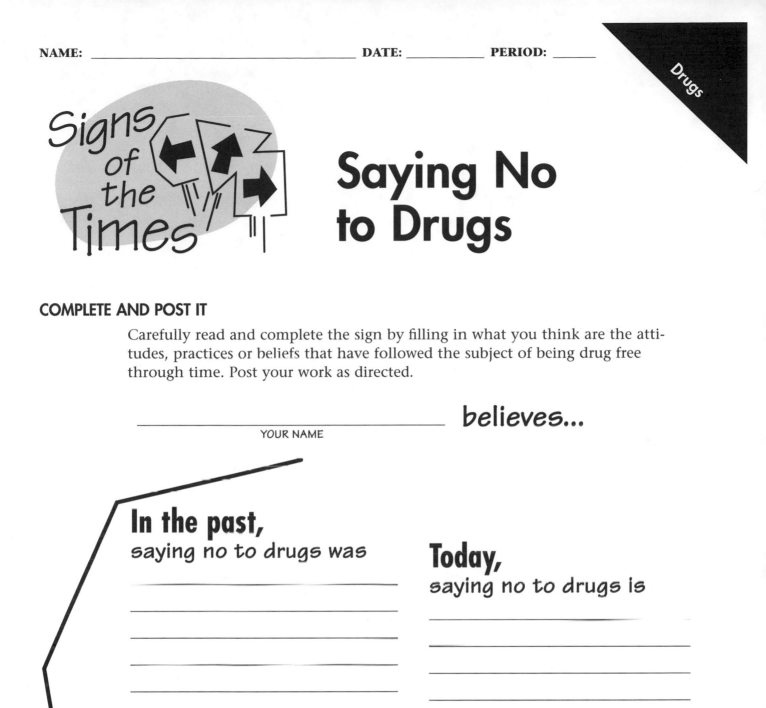

Saying No to Drugs

COMPLETE AND POST IT

Carefully read and complete the sign by filling in what you think are the attitudes, practices or beliefs that have followed the subject of being drug free through time. Post your work as directed.

_____ believes...
YOUR NAME

In the past,
saying no to drugs was
_____
_____
_____
_____

Today,
saying no to drugs is
_____
_____
_____
_____

In the future,
saying no to drugs will probably be
_____
_____
_____

Thinking About Going Along

Tobacco, Alcohol and Drugs

COLLABORATE AND CREATE

As a group, discuss your reactions to and the issues that you identify with the idea of going along. Use the letters of the words creatively to record the key points of your discussion. You might want to work out a rough draft first. Be prepared to post your work and share it with the class.

G _____
O _____
I _____
N _____
G _____

A _____
L _____
O _____
N _____
G _____

A Closer Look at Me

Me and Drugs

READ AND RESPOND

Read the following statements and select a "yes" or "no" response for each. Use the last column to describe evidence of your own personal behavior that supports your answer.

Statements	Yes or No?	My Evidence
1. I recognize the signs of stress in myself.		
2. I have healthy ways to cope with personal stress.		
3. I recognize the dangers of using alcohol and tobacco to relax.		
4. I try to manage pain and discomfort without drugs as often as possible.		
5. I participate in activities that promote being drug free.		

REVIEW AND RESPOND

Review your responses and evidence. Use the back of this sheet to write at least 7 sentences about the profile of you they reveal. Say what you think or feel about this profile and what impact it has on your health and well-being today as well as in the future.

Exploring My Thinking About Drugs

THINK, SELECT AND RESPOND

Use this sheet during your lesson(s) about drugs. At the teacher's signal, select and complete the prompt that best fits your personal thinking at the timc. Be prepared to share your thoughts with others.

I wonder if people who are addicted...

_____
_____
_____
_____
_____

I think a person who uses drugs... _____

_____
_____
_____

I am surprised to hear others say...

_____
_____
_____
_____
_____

Learning about drugs in school is...

_____
_____
_____
_____

Kids will stop get-ting involved with drugs when...

_____
_____
_____
_____
_____

Most people get involved with drugs because...

_____
_____
_____
_____
_____

What adults don't understand about alcohol and teens is...

_____
_____
_____

Tobacco

Courage and Tobacco

THINK AND ANNOTATE

Take a few moments to think about feeling courageous. Annotate the figure to show what this emotion can make a person think, say and do. A sample has been done for you.

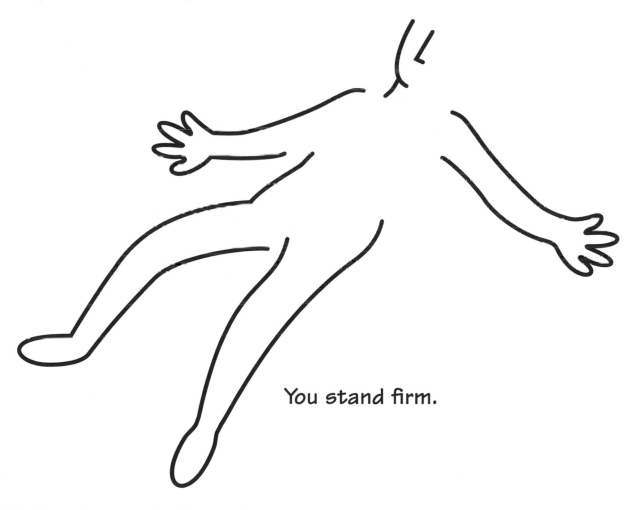

You stand firm.

CONSIDER AND CONCLUDE

State what impact you think courage has on a person's attitude and ability to make healthy choices when faced with pressure to use tobacco. Identify some people and personal actions that could help a person maintain this healthy emotion.

Stress and Alcohol

THINK AND ANNOTATE

Take a few moments to think about feeling stressed. Annotate the figure to show what this emotion can make a person think, say and do. A sample has been done for you.

Sometimes you laugh stuff off.

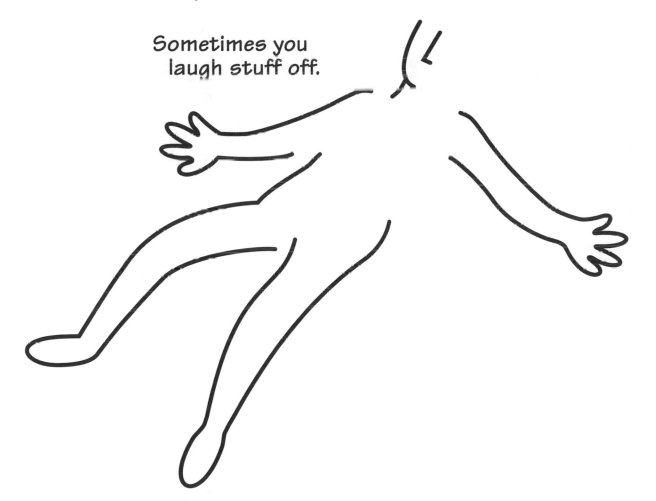

CONSIDER AND CONCLUDE

State what impact you think stress has on a person's attitude and ability to make healthy choices when faced with pressure to use alcohol. Identify some people and personal actions that could help a person cope with this emotion in a healthy way.

Tobacco

Addiction

THINK AND WRITE

Think about how the following word, idea or image relates to the topic of tobacco. Write down your thoughts until you have a reaction that is at least 3–5 sentences long.

_____

_____

_____

_____

_____

_____

_____

_____

COLLABORATE AND WRITE ABOUT IT AGAIN

As a team, begin by sharing your individual responses. Then, using a new sheet of paper and your original writings, compose a single mini-essay that represents the team thoughts, feelings and attitudes about the word or phrase. Be prepared to share your work with the class.

REVIEW AND PROCESS

Discuss your team's essay. Talk about your points of agreement and differences of opinion. What kinds of resolutions does your group essay reflect?

Alcohol

Driving Under the Influence

THINK AND WRITE

Think about how the following phrase, idea or image relates to the topic of alcohol. Write down your thoughts until you have a reaction that is at least 3–5 sentences long.

Driving Under the Influence

_____

_____

_____

_____

_____

_____

_____

_____

_____

COLLABORATE AND WRITE ABOUT IT AGAIN

As a team, begin by sharing your individual responses. Then, using a new sheet of paper and your original writings, compose a single mini-essay that represents the team thoughts, feelings and attitudes about the word or phrase. Be prepared to share your work with the class.

REVIEW AND PROCESS

Discuss your team's essay. Talk about your points of agreement and differences of opinion. What kinds of resolutions does your group essay reflect?

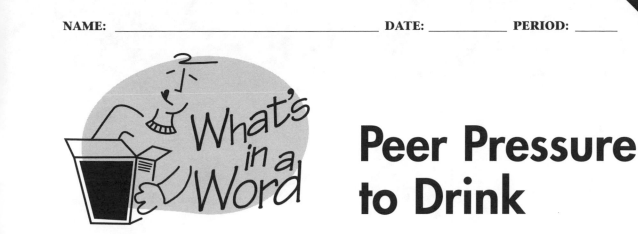

Peer Pressure to Drink

THINK AND WRITE

Think about how the following phrase, idea or image relates to the topic of alcohol. Write down your thoughts until you have a reaction that is at least 3–5 sentences long.

_____

_____

_____

_____

_____

_____

_____

_____

_____

COLLABORATE AND WRITE ABOUT IT AGAIN

As a team, begin by sharing your individual responses. Then, using a new sheet of paper and your original writings, compose a single mini-essay that represents the team thoughts, feelings and attitudes about the word or phrase. Be prepared to share your work with the class.

REVIEW AND PROCESS

Discuss your team's essay. Talk about your points of agreement and differences of opinion. What kinds of resolutions does your group essay reflect?

Drugs

Choosing Not to Use

THINK AND WRITE

Think about how the following phrase, idea or image relates to the topic of drugs. Write down your thoughts until you have a reaction that is at least 3–5 sentences long.

Choosing Not to Use

_____
_____
_____
_____
_____
_____
_____
_____

COLLABORATE AND WRITE ABOUT IT AGAIN

As a team, begin by sharing your individual responses. Then, using a new sheet of paper and your original writings, compose a single mini-essay that represents the team thoughts, feelings and attitudes about the word or phrase. Be prepared to share your work with the class.

REVIEW AND PROCESS

Discuss your team's essay. Talk about your points of agreement and differences of opinion. What kinds of resolutions does your group essay reflect?

Peer View Mirror

Tobacco and Me

SURVEY YOUR PEERS

Use the following questions to survey 3 of your friends or peers on the topic of tobacco use. Use the back of this sheet to record the responses. Use the steps at the bottom of this sheet to tally and discuss your survey results.

SURVEY QUESTIONS

1. At what age were you first offered tobacco?

2. What is your impression of a person your age who smokes?

3. Do you think nicotine is as harmful as other drugs?

ANALYZE AND CONCLUDE

1. As a class, tally the results of your survey questions on the board.

2. Examine the results and discuss any obvious trends, patterns or unexpected responses.

3. For each question, formulate a conclusion based on the responses. Post the conclusions in a visible spot to refer to during this unit of study.

Teens, Alcohol and Me

Alcohol

SURVEY YOUR PEERS

Use the following questions to survey 3 of your friends or peers on the topic of teens and alcohol. Use the back of this sheet to record the responses. Use the steps at the bottom of this sheet to tally and discuss your survey results.

SURVEY QUESTIONS

1. Why do you think teens begin to use alcohol?

2. What will keep them from using it?

3. What do you think about people who pressure their friends to drink?

ANALYZE AND CONCLUDE

1. As a class, tally the results of your survey questions on the board.

2. Examine the results and discuss any obvious trends, patterns or unexpected responses.

3. For each question, formulate a conclusion based on the responses. Post the conclusions in a visible spot to refer to during this unit of study.

Being Courageous and Staying Drug Free

YOUR CHALLENGE

Use what you know and are learning about tobacco, alcohol and other drugs to tell your peers how being courageous can help people choose not to experiment with or use drugs.

THINK ABOUT IT

- Courage is the willingness to face and deal with things that are dangerous or painful rather than withdrawing from them or just giving in.
- Being courageous enough to stand up for your decisions will sometimes make you different from others. That difference may carry a price.
- The courage and choice to be or become drug free may be challenged by peers and friends.

DESIGN AND DELIVER

Using the Challenge and Think About It statements, design and deliver a P.A. system campaign to educate and motivate your peers to call upon personal courage to remain or become drug-free.

PROJECT STEPS

1. Work as a class to brainstorm a list of the kinds of ideas, themes and basic information that would help your peers and friends recognize and value the role being courageous plays in helping people choose not to experiment with or use drugs.

2. Work as collaborative groups to design at least 3 appropriate messages that could be part of a week-long P.A. campaign.

3. As a class, select the best messages and some announcers for the campaign.

4. Practice with the P.A. system after school.

5. Deliver and evaluate the effectiveness of the campaign.

The Call Is For You

Clearing Away the Smoke

COLLABORATE AND ADVISE

As a group, take the phone call of a peer in need of help and advice. Work to problem-solve the scenario assigned to your group. Put yourself in the caller's place. Offer the healthiest advice you can. Be ready to share and discuss your responses with the class.

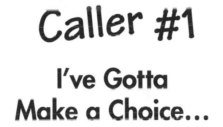

Caller #1

I've Gotta Make a Choice...

I sure am in trouble with my friends. We're all on the team, so we take staying in shape and being healthy seriously. I have this new friend I invited to hang out with us last Friday. The minute we got in the car, my friend lit up a cigarette. The smoke was nasty, and so were the looks I got from the teammate who owns the car. Except for the smoking, my new friend is great to be around. But the word from my group is that I've got a choice to make, my new friend or them. What can I do?

Continued

Continued ....

Tobacco

Clearing Away the Smoke

Caller #2

There's Gonna Be Pressure...

I was hanging out at the mall like I always do, in a cloud of smoke, with all my girlfriends...when it suddenly came home to me. I can't really say why exactly, but it's clear to me that I don't want to smoke anymore. I know that quitting is going to be hard enough without the stuff my group is going to throw at me about being different. I can hear it now. They'll call me a wimp and a "school girl." It's almost enough to make me forget the whole idea. But I gotta try to quit. How can I deal with it?

Clearing Away the Smoke

Caller #3

I Know You'll Agree...

"That's it! You're grounded!" My parents yelled for a while longer and then finally left my room—all because they found a carton of cigarettes in my closet. I need you to help me convince my parents that if I want to smoke it's none of their business. I'm old enough and smart enough to make up my own mind about "smelling like an ashtray" or "dying from cancer." (Like it'll ever happen to me!) Give me some advice on how to get them off my back about this.

Think, Choose, Act Healthy

Clearing Away the Smoke

Caller #4

She's My Girlfriend and I Care...

She's pretty and really smart. I care about her a lot, and I wouldn't do anything to hurt her. But we've got a problem. You see, she smokes. I sometimes think I've gotten used to it, but then it grosses me out when I smell it in her hair and clothes or on her breath when we kiss. Yesterday I was holding her hand, and I noticed that her fingers were looking yellow and old. How can she do this to her body?! She told me she started in grade school, almost 6 years ago. If I tell her I hate it, she'll probably think I don't like her or can't accept her the way she is. Help me out, please.

Decisions About Alcohol

COLLABORATE AND ADVISE

As a group, take the phone call of a peer in need of help and advice. Work to problem-solve the scenario assigned to your group. Put yourself in the caller's place. Offer the healthiest advice you can. Be ready to share and discuss your responses with the class.

Caller #1

Who's the Bigger Fool?

Who's the bigger fool? Me, because I thought I could drink and drive, or my friends who agreed to get into a car with a drunk driver? If that other driver hadn't swerved and there'd been more cars on the road, I think I would have killed myself and my friends! And, afterwards, we all pretended it was no big deal. We even laughed about it.

Now that I've really thought about it, I've tried to talk about it with them, but they just shrug it off. What can I say to make them face what almost happened? How can I make sure I never find myself in that kind of situation again—as a driver or a passenger?

Tobacco

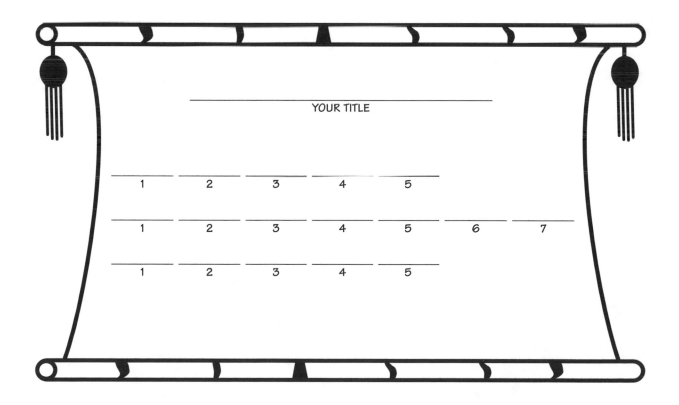

Secondhand Smoke

THINK, FOCUS AND EXPRESS

Using haiku format, compose a poem about secondhand smoke. Present the issues, images or emotions that you think are a part of this challenge. Use the form below to help you write your haiku. Be ready to read and post your work.

Haiku

Five short syl-la-bles,
then fol-low with sev-en more.
Five a-gain, the end.

YOUR TITLE

  1   2   3   4   5

  1   2   3   4   5   6   7

  1   2   3   4   5

Good Times Without Alcohol

THINK, FOCUS AND EXPRESS

Using haiku format, compose a poem about good times without alcohol. Present the issues, images or emotions that you think are a part of this challenge. Use the form below to help you write your haiku. Be ready to read and post your work.

Haiku

Five short syl-la-bles,
then fol-low with sev-en more.
Five a-gain, the end.

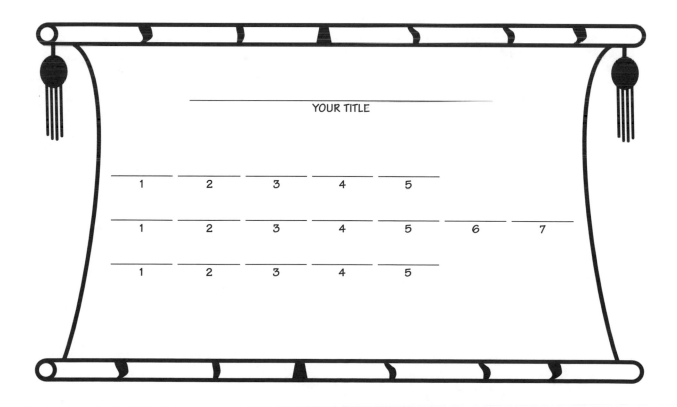

How to Resist Peer Pressure

THINK AND PRESCRIBE

Consider all you know about the importance of being able to resist peer pressure to use tobacco, alcohol and other drugs. Generate a list of tips or advice to help people refuse offers of drugs from both friends and strangers.

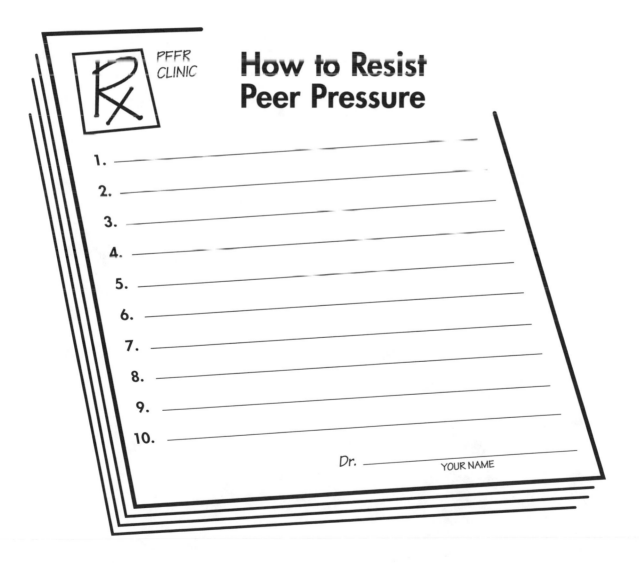

Rx PFFR CLINIC

How to Resist Peer Pressure

1. _____
2. _____
3. _____
4. _____
5. _____
6. _____
7. _____
8. _____
9. _____
10. _____

Dr. _____ YOUR NAME

Violence and Injury

Thinking and Talking About Injury Prevention

ASK, LISTEN AND LEARN

Use 1 of the following questions as a **Question Roll Call** prompt (modify if needed). Write the selected question on the board and ask students to think about a response. Call roll. Students use their answer to the question to replace the traditional response of "here" or "present."

Risks

1. What is an example of a positive risk?

2. What is an example of an unsafe risk?

3. What was the last injury you suffered? Could it have been avoided?

4. Do guys or girls take dangerous risks more often? Why?

5. Why do young people think that nothing bad will ever happen to them?

Relationship Violence

6. What can make a date a setting for relationship violence?

7. What advice would help keep people safe before or during a date?

8. How does sexual reputation affect people's expectations of each other?

9. React to the statement: "Rape is not about sex, it's about power."

10. What role does the media play in our view of relationship violence?

Stress and Suicide

11. Name something that stresses you out on a daily basis.

12. Name something that stresses you out every now and then.

13. How do you behave under major stress?

14. How do you cope with mild stress?

15. How do you cope with major stress?

Face to Face

Illusions

READ, THINK AND DISCUSS

> People look at us and think,
> "What a great couple they make...
> You can tell they really care for each other...It shows!"
> Maybe it's the way we're practically glued together
> That "Don't stray too far from my sight" stuff...
> Or it could be the way that arm slips around my waist
> when anyone else gets too close...
> It's just showing people how it is with us...
> But it's really not that way at all.
> Would you still think it was sweet if you knew
> that the whispers I hear aren't, "I'd do anything for you..."
> but, "I'll do anything *to you*..."
> What did you ask? Prom? Oh yeah...the prom...
> Who else would I go with?
> Who else *could* I go with...

CONSTRUCT YOUR OWN MEANING

As a class, discuss the reading by first sharing your initial reactions. Then identify the issues involved in this situation.

Signs of the Times

Taking a Risk

COMPLETE AND POST IT

Carefully read and complete the sign by filling in what you think are some of the attitudes, practices or beliefs that have followed the subject of risk taking through time. Post your work as directed.

_____ **believes...**
YOUR NAME

In the past,
taking a risk was
_____
_____
_____
_____
_____

Today, taking a risk is
_____
_____
_____
_____
_____

In the future,
taking a risk will probably be
_____
_____
_____

How Music Moves Us

COMPLETE AND POST IT

Carefully read and complete the sign by filling in what you think are some of the attitudes, practices or beliefs that have followed the subject of how music influences people's behavior through time. Post your work as directed.

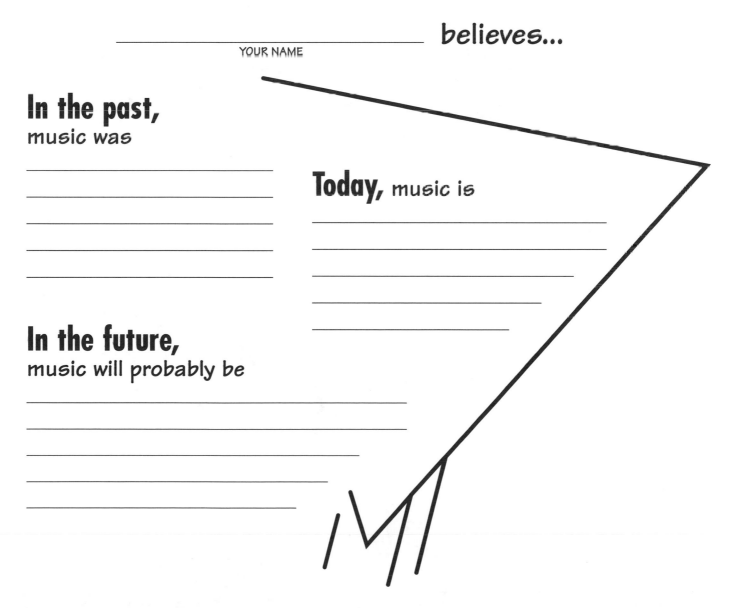

_____ **believes...**
YOUR NAME

In the past,
music was

_____

_____

_____

_____

Today, music is

_____

_____

_____

_____

_____

In the future,
music will probably be

_____

_____

_____

_____

_____

Signs of the Times

Coping

COMPLETE AND POST IT

Carefully read and complete the sign by filling in what you think are some of the attitudes, practices or beliefs that have followed the subject of coping through time. Post your work as directed.

_____ **believes...**
YOUR NAME

In the past, *coping was*

_____
_____
_____
_____
_____

Today, *coping is*

_____
_____
_____
_____
_____

In the future,
coping will probably be

_____
_____
_____

Violence

Thinking About School Fights

COLLABORATE AND CREATE

As a group, discuss your reactions to and the issues you identify with fights at school. Use the letters of the words creatively to record the key points of your discussion. You might want to work out a rough draft first. Be prepared to post your work and share it with the class.

S _____
C _____
H _____
O _____
O _____
L _____
F _____
I _____
G _____
H _____
T _____
S _____

Thinking About Gangs

COLLABORATE AND CREATE

As a group, discuss your reactions to and the issues you identify with gangs. Use the letters of the words creatively to record the key points of your discussion. You might want to work out a rough draft first. Be prepared to post your work and share it with the class.

G _____

A _____

N _____

G _____

S _____

Me and Violence

READ AND RESPOND

Read the statements and select a "yes" or "no" response for each. Use the last column to describe evidence of your own personal behavior that supports your answer.

Statements	Yes or No?	My Evidence
1. I express anger and frustration in a healthy way.		
2. I am good at spotting conflict in its early stages.		
3. I don't believe you have to fight to prove yourself.		
4. I surround myself with friends who make it easy not to fight.		
5. I actively promote nonviolence among others.		

REVIEW AND RESPOND

Review your responses and evidence. Use the back of this sheet to write at least 7 sentences about the profile of you they reveal. Say what you think or feel about this profile and what impact it has on your health and well-being today as well as in the future.

Suicide

Me and Suicide

READ AND RESPOND

Read the statements and select a "yes" or "no" response for each. Use the last column to describe evidence of your own personal behavior that supports your answer.

Statements	Yes or No?	My Evidence
1. I can recognize and cope with feelings of sadness or loss.		
2. I have healthy ways to cope with frustration.		
3. I have a good friend I can talk to in tough times.		
4. I know when it is time to get help with my problems.		
5. I would know where to find help for someone who was talking and thinking about suicide.		

REVIEW AND RESPOND

Review your responses and evidence. Use the back of this sheet to write at least 7 sentences about the profile of you they reveal. Say what you think or feel about this profile and what impact it has on your health and well-being today as well as in the future.

Think, Choose, Act Healthy

Violence and Injury **329**

Exploring My Thinking About Violence and Injury

THINK, SELECT AND RESPOND

Use this sheet during your lesson(s) about violence or injury. At the teacher's signal, select and complete the prompt that best fits your personal thinking at the time. Be prepared to share your thoughts with others.

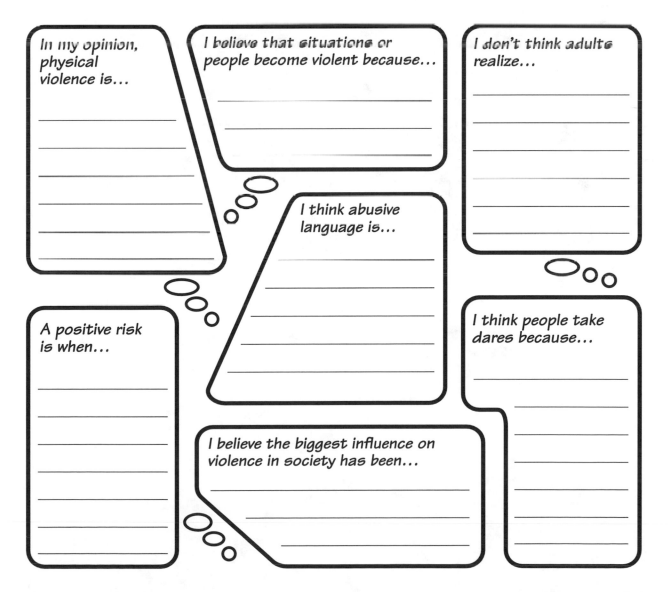

In my opinion, physical violence is...

I believe that situations or people become violent because...

I don't think adults realize...

I think abusive language is...

A positive risk is when...

I think people take dares because...

I believe the biggest influence on violence in society has been...

Suicide

Exploring My Thinking About Suicide

THINK, SELECT AND RESPOND

Use this sheet during your lesson(s) about suicide. At the teacher's signal, select and complete the prompt that best fits your personal thinking at the time. Be prepared to share your thoughts with others.

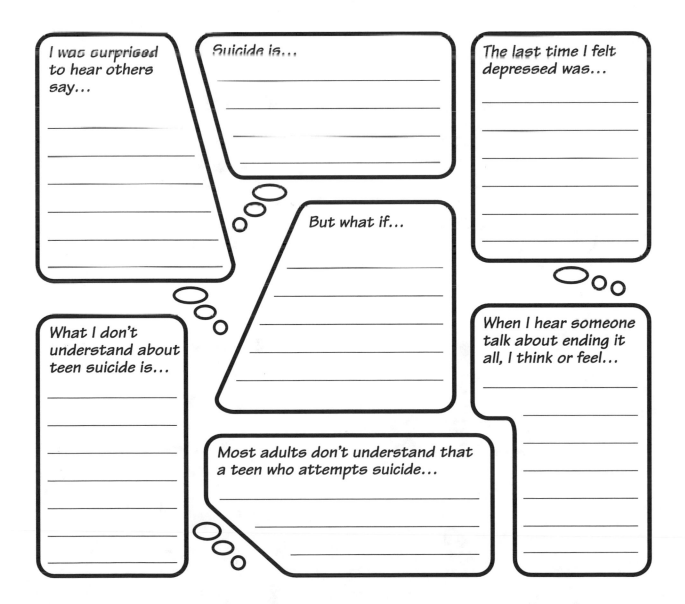

I was surprised to hear others say...

Suicide is...

The last time I felt depressed was...

But what if...

What I don't understand about teen suicide is...

When I hear someone talk about ending it all, I think or feel...

Most adults don't understand that a teen who attempts suicide...

Think, Choose, Act Healthy

Curiosity and Personal Safety

THINK AND ANNOTATE

Take a few moments to think about curiosity. Annotate the figure to show what this emotion can make a person think, say and do. A sample has been done for you.

You take a closer look at something or someone.

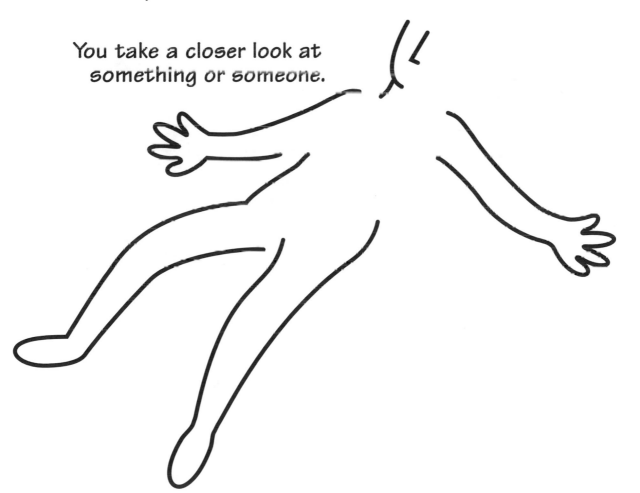

CONSIDER AND CONCLUDE

State what impact you think curiosity has on a person's attitude and ability to make healthy choices about taking risks. Identify some people and personal actions that could help a person cope with this emotion in a healthy way.

Think, Choose, Act Healthy

Anger and Violence

THINK AND ANNOTATE

Take a few moments to think about anger. Annotate the figure to show what this emotion can make a person think, say and do. A sample has been done for you.

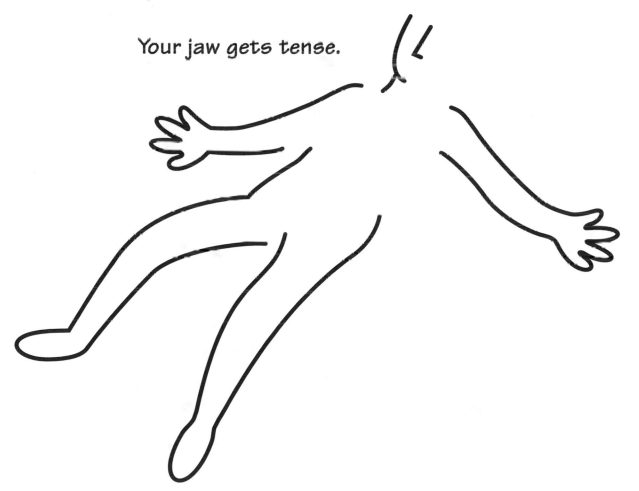

Your jaw gets tense.

CONSIDER AND CONCLUDE

State what impact you think anger has on a person's attitude and ability to make healthy choices in situations that have the potential for conflict or violence. Identify some people and personal actions that could help a person cope with this emotion in a healthy way.

Think, Choose, Act Healthy

Anatomy of an Emotion

Depression and Suicide

THINK AND ANNOTATE

Take a few moments to think about depression. Annotate the figure to show what this emotion can make a person think, say and do. A sample has been done for you.

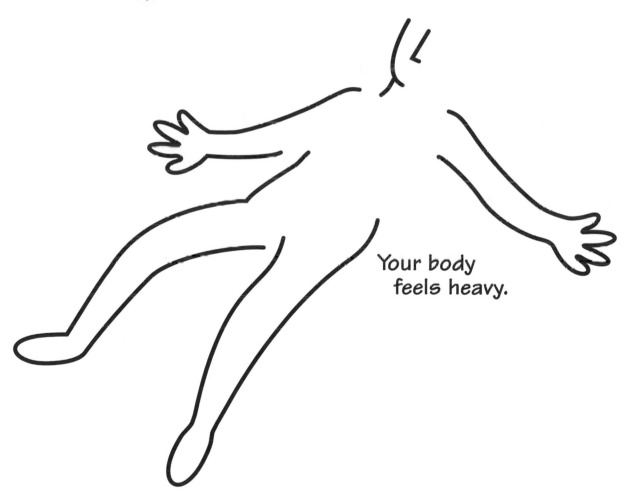

Your body feels heavy.

CONSIDER AND CONCLUDE

State what impact you think depression has on a person's attitude and ability to make healthy choices about how to cope with feelings of being down or helpless. Identify some people and personal actions that could help a person cope with this emotion in a healthy way.

What's in a Word

Being a Victim

THINK AND WRITE

Think about how the following phrase, idea or image relates to the topic of violence. Write down your thoughts until you have a reaction that is at least 3–5 sentences long.

_____

_____

_____

_____

_____

_____

_____

_____

_____

COLLABORATE AND WRITE ABOUT IT AGAIN

As a team, begin by sharing your individual responses. Then, using a new sheet of paper and your original writings, compose a single mini-essay that represents the team thoughts, feelings and attitudes about the word or phrase. Be prepared to share your work with the class.

REVIEW AND PROCESS

Discuss your team's essay. Talk about your points of agreement and differences of opinion. What kinds of resolutions does your group essay reflect?

Violence

Date Rape

THINK AND WRITE

Think about how the following phrase, idea or image relates to the topic of violence. Write down your thoughts until you have a reaction that is at least 3–5 sentences long.

_____

_____

_____

_____

_____

_____

_____

_____

_____

COLLABORATE AND WRITE ABOUT IT AGAIN

As a team, begin by sharing your individual responses. Then, using a new sheet of paper and your original writings, compose a single mini-essay that represents the team thoughts, feelings and attitudes about the word or phrase. Be prepared to share your work with the class.

REVIEW AND PROCESS

Discuss your team's essay. Talk about your points of agreement and differences of opinion. What kinds of resolutions does your group essay reflect?

Nonviolence

THINK AND WRITE

Think about how the following word, idea or image relates to the topic of violence. Write down your thoughts until you have a reaction that is at least 3–5 sentences long.

_____
_____
_____
_____
_____
_____
_____
_____
_____

COLLABORATE AND WRITE ABOUT IT AGAIN

As a team, begin by sharing your individual responses. Then, using a new sheet of paper and your original writings, compose a single mini-essay that represents the team thoughts, feelings and attitudes about the word or phrase. Be prepared to share your work with the class.

REVIEW AND PROCESS

Discuss your team's essay. Talk about your points of agreement and differences of opinion. What kinds of resolutions does your group essay reflect?

Teen Suicide

THINK AND WRITE

Think about how the following phrase, idea or image relates to the topics of violence and injury prevention. Write down your thoughts until you have a reaction that is at least 3–5 sentences long.

_____
_____
_____
_____
_____
_____
_____
_____
_____
_____

COLLABORATE AND WRITE ABOUT IT AGAIN

As a team, begin by sharing your individual responses. Then, using a new sheet of paper and your original writings, compose a single mini-essay that represents the team thoughts, feelings and attitudes about the word or phrase. Be prepared to share your work with the class.

REVIEW AND PROCESS

Discuss your team's essay. Talk about your points of agreement and differences of opinion. What kinds of resolutions does your group essay reflect?

Risks and Me

SURVEY YOUR PEERS

Use the following questions to interview 3 of your friends or peers on the topic of risks. Use the back of this sheet to record the responses. Use the steps at the bottom of this sheet to tally and discuss your survey results.

SURVEY QUESTIONS

1. How long ago did you take a risk that endangered your health?

2. Were you alone when you took the risk or were you with friends?

3. What do you think motivates people to take harmful risks?

ANALYZE AND CONCLUDE

1. As a class, tally the results of your survey questions on the board.

2. Examine the results and discuss any obvious trends, patterns or unexpected responses.

3. For each question, formulate a conclusion based on the responses. Post the conclusions in a visible spot to refer to during this unit of study.

Peer View Mirror

Sexual Harassment and Me

SURVEY YOUR PEERS

Use the following questions to interview 3 of your friends or peers on the topic of sexual harassment. Use the back of this sheet to record the responses. Use the steps at the bottom of this sheet to tally and discuss your survey results.

SURVEY QUESTIONS

1. Does our school have a sexual harassment problem?

2. Where on this school campus can a person go to get help?

3. What can be done to prevent sexual harassment?

ANALYZE AND CONCLUDE

1. As a class, tally the results of your survey questions on the board.

2. Examine the results and discuss any obvious trends, patterns or unexpected responses.

3. For each question, formulate a conclusion based on the responses. Post the conclusions in a visible spot to refer to during this unit of study.

Being Fair and Dealing with Conflict

YOUR CHALLENGE

Use what you know and are learning about violence to tell your peers how being fair can help people avoid or solve conflict in a nonviolent manner.

THINK ABOUT IT

- Being fair means "doing the right thing," even when tempted to take the easy or vengeful way out.
- Being fair means valuing and acting with consideration for other people's points of view.
- Being fair requires the ability to think, reason, communicate and, when needed, to manage strong emotions.

DESIGN AND DELIVER

Using the Challenge and Think About It statements, design and deliver a P.A. system campaign to educate and motivate your peers to call upon a personal sense of fairness to avoid and solve conflict in a nonviolent manner.

PROJECT STEPS

1. Work as a class to brainstorm a list of the kinds of ideas, themes and basic information that would help your peers and friends recognize and value the role being fair plays in avoiding or solving conflict in a nonviolent manner.

2. Work as collaborative groups to design at least 3 appropriate messages that could be part of a week-long P.A. campaign.

3. As a class, select the best messages and some announcers for the campaign.

4. Practice with the P.A. system after school.

5. Deliver and evaluate the effectiveness of the campaign.

The Media Connection

COLLABORATE AND ADVISE

As a group, take the phone call of a peer in need of help and advice. Work to problem-solve the scenario assigned to your group. Put yourself in the caller's place. Offer the healthiest advice you can. Be ready to share and discuss your responses with the class.

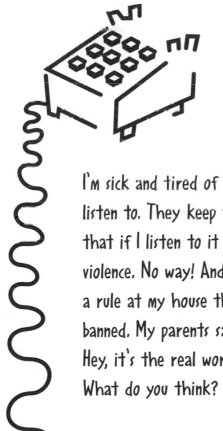

Caller #1

Turn That Junk Off!

I'm sick and tired of people raggin' on me because of the kind of music I listen to. They keep telling me how graphic and violent it is. They say that if I listen to it long enough it'll warp me and make me numb to real violence. No way! And videos—don't even get me started on that! There's a rule at my house that certain programs on the music video channel are banned. My parents say they're a bad influence on my little brother. Hey, it's the real world, and he's got to learn about it sometime. What do you think?

Continued

The Media Connection?

Caller #2

Have You Really Been Watching?

Sometimes I feel I'm fighting a losing battle. People say, "What makes you think you can change things?" But I can't sit by and not say something about the violence and disrespect that's shown on TV and in movies today. I really believe it repeats itself in the real world—our world. All you need to do is look at what's happening around you. Watch how people react to and treat each other. Listen to the put-downs, watch the news, read the papers. Then try to tell me I'm wrong. Better yet, tell me what you and I can do about it!

The Cry for Help

COLLABORATE AND ADVISE

As a group, take the phone call of a peer in need of help and advice. Work to problem-solve the scenario assigned to your group. Put yourself in the caller's place. Offer the healthiest advice you can. Be ready to share and discuss your responses with the rest of the class.

Caller #1

No One Cares...

No one cares or has the time even to think about what happens to me. I'm tired of trying to make my life work. I'm tired of people not being able to give me answers. Suicide isn't something I would ever do...but maybe if I just pretended I was thinking about it...Then maybe people would notice me. What would be wrong with doing that? It's not like it would hurt anybody or anything! Tell me what you think.

The Cry for Help

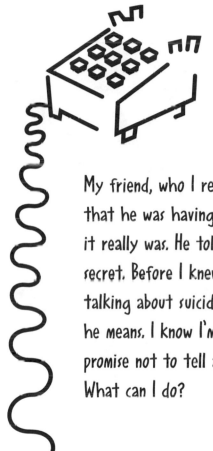

Caller #2

Boxed into a Corner...

My friend, who I really care about, has boxed me into a corner. I knew that he was having a rough time but I guess I wasn't tuned in to how bad it really was. He told me he needed to talk to someone who could keep a secret. Before I knew what I was promising, I was in over my head. He's talking about suicide! He hasn't said those exact words, but it's what he means. I know I'm not the best person to help him, but he made me promise not to tell anyone else. I'm between a rock and a hard place. What can I do?

Accepting Differences

THINK, FOCUS AND EXPRESS

Using haiku format, compose a poem about accepting differences. Present the issues, images or emotions that you think are a part of this challenge. Use the form below to help you write your haiku. Be ready to read and post your work.

Haiku

Five short syl-la-bles,
then fol-low with sev-en more.
Five a-gain, the end.

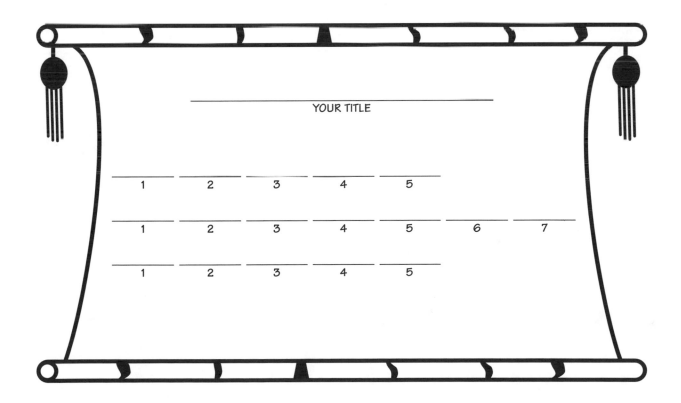

YOUR TITLE

1	2	3	4	5
1	2	3	4	5	6	7
1	2	3	4	5

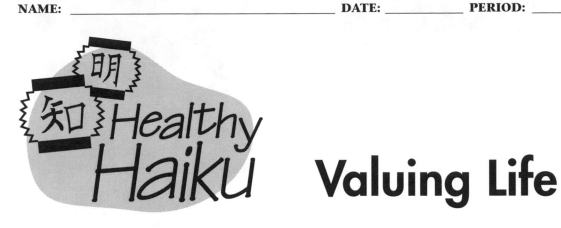

Valuing Life

THINK, FOCUS AND EXPRESS

Using haiku format, compose a poem about valuing life. Present the issues, images or emotions that you think are a part of this challenge. Use the form below to help you write your haiku. Be ready to read and post your work.

Haiku

Five short syl-la-bles,
then fol-low with sev-en more.
Five a-gain, the end.

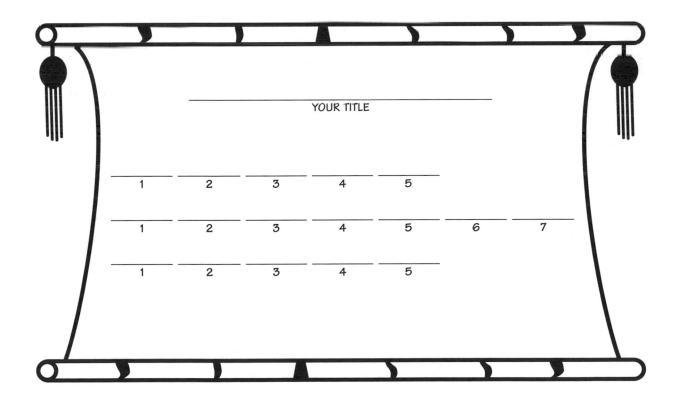

YOUR TITLE

1	2	3	4	5		
1	2	3	4	5	6	7
1	2	3	4	5		

How to Stay Cool in Hot Situations

THINK AND PRESCRIBE

Consider what you know about the importance of being able to manage strong emotions like anger, frustration or jealousy. Generate a list of tips or advice for keeping a cool head in situations that might create these kinds of feelings.

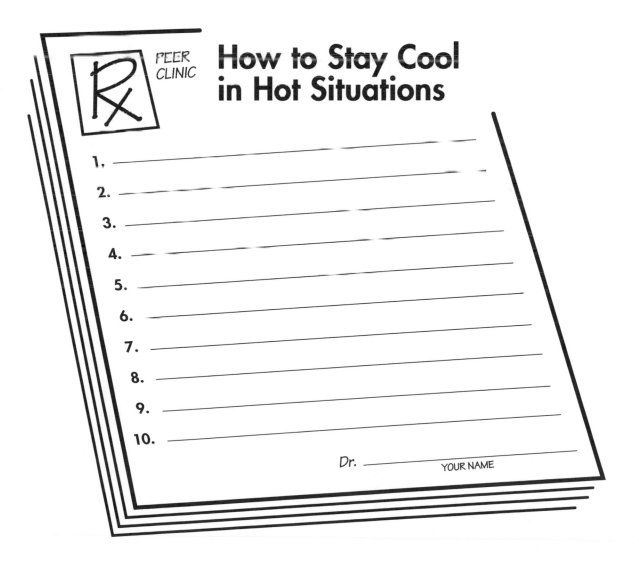

How to Stay Cool in Hot Situations

PEER CLINIC

1. _____
2. _____
3. _____
4. _____
5. _____
6. _____
7. _____
8. _____
9. _____
10. _____

Dr. _____
YOUR NAME

How to Stop Sexual Harassment

THINK AND PRESCRIBE

Consider all you know about the problem of sexual harassment. Generate a list of tips or advice that will help both men and women diminish and stop this problem.

PEER CLINIC

How to Stop Sexual Harassment

1. _____
2. _____
3. _____
4. _____
5. _____
6. _____
7. _____
8. _____
9. _____
10. _____

Dr. _____
YOUR NAME

Steps Toward My Future

Being Nonviolent

CONSIDER, GENERATE AND APPLY

Think about the healthy goal in the center of the activity sheet. List as many resources and behaviors as you can think of that will help you build your path toward this goal. Use this information to complete the "steps" on the next page. Share and discuss your work. Finalize your responses and post your activity sheet as directed.

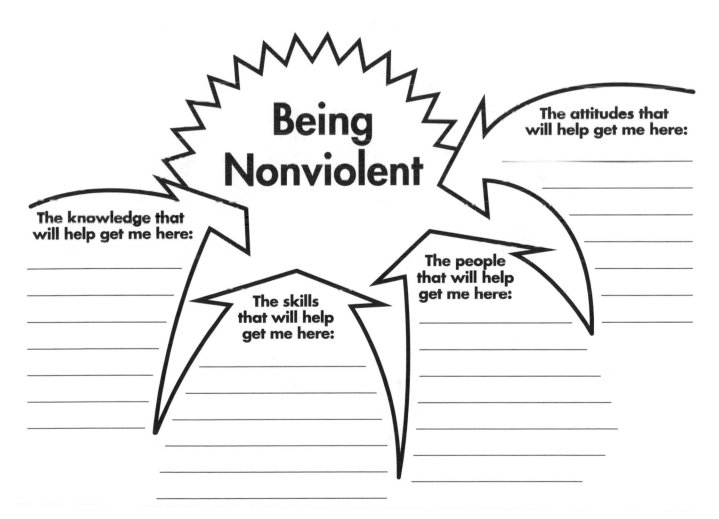

Being Nonviolent

The attitudes that will help get me here:

The knowledge that will help get me here:

The people that will help get me here:

The skills that will help get me here: